The Iran-Iraq War

Titles in the World History Series

The Abolition of American Slavery
The Age of Augustus
The Age of Exploration
The Age of Feudalism
The Age of Napoléon
The Age of Pericles
The Alamo
America in the 1960s
The American Revolution
Ancient America
Ancient Chinese Dynasties
Ancient Greece
The Ancient Near East
The Assyrian Empire
The Battle of the
    Little Bighorn
The Black Death
The Byzantine Empire
Building the Transcontinental Railroad
Caesar's Conquest of Gaul
The California Gold Rush
The Chinese Cultural
    Revolution
The Civil Rights Movement
The Cold War
The Collapse of the
    Roman Republic
Colonial America
The Computer Revolution
The Conquest of Mexico
The Constitution and the
    Founding of America
The Crimean War
The Cuban Missile Crisis
The Early Middle Ages
Egypt of the Pharaohs
The Enlightenment
The Great Depression
Greek and Roman Mythology
Greek and Roman Science

Greek and Roman Sport
Greek and Roman Theater
The History of Medicine
The History of Rock & Roll
The History of Slavery
The Incan Empire
The Internment of the Japanese
The Iran-Iraq War
The Italian Renaissance
The Late Middle Ages
The Making of the Atom Bomb
The Mayan Civilization
The Mexican-American War
The Mexican Revolution
The Mexican War of
    Independence
The Mongol Empire
The Persian Empire
Prohibition
The Punic Wars
The Reagan Years
The Reformation
The Renaissance
The Rise and Fall of the
    Soviet Union
The Roaring Twenties
Roosevelt and the
    New Deal
Russia of the Tsars
The Salem Witch Trials
The Space Race
The Spanish-American War
The Stone Age
The Titanic
Traditional Africa
Twentieth-Century Science
Viking Conquests
The War of 1812
World War II in the Pacific

WORLD HISTORY SERIES ▪▪▪

The Iran-Iraq War

by
David Schaffer

LUCENT BOOKS®

THOMSON
GALE™

San Diego • Detroit • New York • San Francisco • Cleveland • New Haven, Conn. • Waterville, Maine • London • Munich

THOMSON
＊
™
GALE

To Ken J.—Peace

© 2003 by Lucent Books. Lucent Books is an imprint of The Gale Group, Inc.,
a division of Thomson Learning, Inc.

Lucent Books® and Thomson Learning™ are trademarks used herein under license.

For more information, contact
Lucent Books
27500 Drake Rd.
Farmington Hills, MI 48331-3535
Or you can visit our Internet site at http://www.gale.com

LIBRARY OF CONGRESS CATALOGING-IN-PUBLICATION DATA

Schaffer, David.
   The Iran-Iraq War / by David Schaffer.
      p. cm. — (World history series)
Includes bibliographical references and index.
   ISBN 1-59018-184-0
   1. Persian Gulf War, 1991—Juvenile literature. [1. Persian Gulf War, 1991.] I. Title.
II. Series.
   DFS79.723 .S33 2003
   956.7044'2—dc21

                                                                 2002006299

Printed in the United States of America

Contents

Foreword

Each year on the first day of school, nearly every history teacher faces the task of explaining why his or her students should study history. One logical answer to this question is that exploring what happened in our past explains how the things we often take for granted—our customs, ideas, and institutions—came to be. As statesman and historian Winston Churchill put it, "Every nation or group of nations has its own tale to tell. Knowledge of the trials and struggles is necessary to all who would comprehend the problems, perils, challenges, and opportunities which confront us today." Thus, a study of history puts modern ideas and institutions in perspective. For example, though the founders of the United States were talented and creative thinkers, they clearly did not invent the concept of democracy. Instead, they adapted some democratic ideas that had originated in ancient Greece and with which the Romans, the British, and others had experimented. An exploration of these cultures, then, reveals their very real connection to us through institutions that continue to shape our daily lives.

Another reason often given for studying history is the idea that lessons exist in the past from which contemporary societies can benefit and learn. This idea, although controversial, has always been an intriguing one for historians. Those who agree that society can benefit from the past often quote philosopher George Santayana's famous statement, "Those who cannot remember the past are condemned to repeat it." Historians who subscribe to Santayana's philosophy believe that, for example, studying the events that led up to the major world wars or other significant historical events would allow society to chart a different and more favorable course in the future.

Just as difficult as convincing students of the importance of studying history is the search for useful and interesting supplementary materials that present historical events in a context that can be easily understood. The volumes in Lucent Books' World History Series attempt to present a broad, balanced, and penetrating view of the march of history. Ancient Egypt's important wars and rulers, for example, are presented against the rich and colorful backdrop of Egyptian religious, social, and cultural developments. The series engages the reader by enhancing historical events with these cultural contexts. For example, in *Ancient Greece*, the text covers the role of women in that society. Slavery is discussed in *The Roman Empire*, as well as how slaves earned their freedom. The numerous and varied aspects of everyday life in these and other societies are explored in each volume of the series. Additionally, the series covers the major political, cultural, and philosophical ideas as the torch of civilization is passed from ancient Mesopotamia and Egypt, through Greece, Rome, Medieval Europe, and other world cultures, to the modern day.

The material in the series is formatted in a thorough, precise, and organized manner. Each volume offers the reader a comprehensive and clearly written overview of an important historical event or period. The topic under discussion is placed in a broad, historical context. For example, *The Italian Renaissance* begins with a discussion of the High Middle Ages and the loss of central control that allowed certain Italian cities to develop artistically. The book ends by looking forward to the Reformation and interpreting the societal changes that grew out of the Renaissance. Thus, students are not only involved in an historical era, but also enveloped by the events leading up to that era and the events following it.

One important and unique feature in the World History Series is the primary and secondary source quotations that richly supplement each volume. These quotes are useful in a number of ways. First, they allow students access to sources they would not normally be exposed to because of the difficulty and obscurity of the original source. The quotations range from interesting anecdotes to farsighted cultural perspectives and are drawn from historical witnesses both past and present. Second, the quotes demonstrate how and where historians themselves derive their information on the past as they strive to reach a consensus on historical events. Lastly, all of the quotes are footnoted, familiarizing students with the citation process and allowing them to verify quotes and/or look up the original source if the quote piques their interest.

Finally, the books in the World History Series provide a detailed launching point for further research. Each book contains a bibliography specifically geared toward student research. A second, annotated bibliography introduces students to all the sources the author consulted when compiling the book. A chronology of important dates gives students an overview, at a glance, of the topic covered. Where applicable, a glossary of terms is included.

In short, the series is designed not only to acquaint readers with the basics of history, but also to make them aware that their lives are a part of an ongoing human saga. Perhaps then they will come to the same realization as famed historian Arnold Toynbee. In his monumental work, *A Study of History*, he wrote about becoming aware of history flowing through him in a mighty current, and of his own life "welling like a wave in the flow of this vast tide."

IMPORTANT DATES DURING
THE IRAN-IRAQ WAR

1978
Ayatollah Khomeini expelled from Iraq and relocates in France; anti-Shah sentiment in Iran intensifies.

1941–1945
Allies in World War II occupy both Iran and Iraq.

1975
Iran and Iraq sign Algiers Accord, resolving many points of conflict between them.

1981
Iranian ground offensives begin to recapture territory taken by Iraq.

1945–1951
Iran and Iraq enjoy period of improved relations, enter into international diplomatic and military agreements.

1968
Baath Socialist Party takes power in Iraq.

1965
Ayatollah Ruhollah Khomeini exiled from Iran.

1945	1950	1955	1960	1975	1980

1953
Reza Shah Pahlavi flees Iran after a popular uprising, but is restored to power by Western nations, especially the United State, after several days.

1971–1972
Relations between Iran and Iraq worsen dramatically, due to disputes over Iran's seizing of Arab-inhabited islands, a friendship treaty between Iraq and Soviet Union, and Iran's disavowal of previous agreements regarding territorial division of the Shatt al Arab.

1979
(Jan.–Feb.) Shah Pahlavi flees Iran; Ayatollah Khomeini becomes head of a new Islamic republican government; (July) Saddam Hussein assumes sole ruling power in Iraq.

1958
The first of three revolutions in the next ten years in Iraq replaces a pro-Western monarchy with a nationalistic, nonaligned republic.

1980
(April) Armed skirmishes break out along the border; (Sept.) Hussein makes televised speech denouncing Iran and refuting Algiers Accord; Iraqi forces invade Iran; (Nov.) Iraqi forces capture city of Khorramshahr in Khuzestan and lay siege to other key Iranian cities.

1982
(Feb.–May) Iran retakes Khorramshahr and breaks the sieges of other key southern cities; (June) Hussein offers to withdraw all Iraqi troops from Iranian territory, but leaves some forces there; (July) Iran invades Iraq; Shia militants make assassination attempt against Hussein; (Nov.) United States removes Iraq from list of nations suspected of sponsoring terrorism, making arms sales to Iraq by American companies more feasible.

1983
(July) Iran makes significant territorial gains in offensive in Iraqi Kurdistan; Iraq uses chemical weapons for the first time in the war; (Dec.) terrorist bombings in Kuwait, an Iraqi war ally, believed to have been carried out with the help of Iranian militants.

1984
(Feb.) Iran's Majnoon offensive captures strategic islands in southeastern Iraqi marshes; (Feb.–June) the War of the Cities draws new mediation efforts from UN Secretary General; (April) Iraq starts targeting ships of nations trading with Iran.

1985
(March) Iran briefly captures the Basra-Baghdad highway; (May) assassination attempt against Kuwait's monarch leads to new Iraqi air and missile attacks on Iranian towns; Iranian retaliation focuses on shelling Basra and missile attacks against other Iraqi towns.

1985	1990	1995	2000

1990
(Aug.) After two years of talks, Iran and Iraq reach permanent peace settlement.

1988
(July) United States shoots down Iranian passenger jet by mistake; Iran unconditionally accepts UN Security Council Resolution 598 two weeks later; (Aug.) Iraq also unconditionally accepts Resolution 598; armed hostilities between Iran and Iraq end.

1987
(May) Iraqi missile accidentally hits naval frigate USS *Stark*; U.S. forces placed on higher alert and instructed to fire on any craft suspected of hostile intentions; (Aug.) Iran makes significant movement in its negotiation position by accepting all points of UN Security Council Resolution 598, but refuses to accept a cease-fire without a simultaneous inquiry into who started the war.

1986
(Feb.) Iran's Fao offensive captures over three hundred square miles on strategic peninsula in southern Iraq; (Oct.) Kuwait requests protection for its oil tankers from Soviet Union and United States; (Nov.) news reports claim United States has been secretly selling arms to Iran; Iran-contra scandal results.

The Persian Gulf, Global Hot Spot

On April 18, 1984, a Panamanian oil tanker sailing through the Persian Gulf was struck by bombs dropped from Iraqi warplanes. Over the next few years, oil tankers from various nations, including Turkey, Liberia, Saudi Arabia, Kuwait, Britain, the Soviet Union, and the United States, would be the victims of naval and air attacks by the armed forces of Iran and Iraq. At the time of the attack on the Panamanian tanker, these two Persian Gulf nations had been at war with each other for almost four years, that war was destined to last just over four years more.

While officially no other nations became participants in what came to be called the Iran-Iraq War, many nations had a vital interest in the conflict, due mostly to the world's dependence on oil from the Persian Gulf region. Some nations favored one side or the other to varying degrees, while others maintained strict neutrality. But regardless of who, if anyone, they supported in the war, many nations suffered adverse effects from that conflict.

DAMAGE AND DESTRUCTION

For some nations, the damage to their oil shipping was only one of the results of the war. Other consequences included damaged prestige as secret arms dealings with Iran or Iraq came to light, touching off political scandals at home. For some other noncombatants, attacks by terrorists allied with Iran or Iraq brought the war home in a very real sense. Furthermore, the war and the way other nations responded to it would fuel militancy and unrest in the Middle East that would plague the world for decades.

While many nations suffered in various ways as a result of the war, by far and away it was Iran and Iraq themselves who incurred the greatest toll in terms of injuries, lost lives, destruction of property, and money spent on weapons. The Iran-Iraq War was the longest war fought directly between two nations during the twentieth century. The war was fought using some of the most modern and devastating weapons in existence. At least one side used chemical weapons, providing a grisly demonstration of the horror that these agents of destruction can visit on combatants. Due in part to the nature of the weapons used, the final combined casualty count of the war between Iran and Iraq exceeded 1 million, of which more than half a million were fatalities. Meanwhile, the total war-related costs have been estimated as being at least $400 billion.

To a significant extent, the war was fueled by personal animosity between the respective heads of state in Iran and Iraq at that time. International journalist and author Robin Wright points to "deepening ideological differences and a personal feud between two men"[1] as being among the causes of the war. Iran was governed by Ayatollah Ruhollah Khomeini, a fundamentalist Muslim cleric who had come to power in a revolution in 1979. Khomeini was bitterly hostile toward Iraq's ruler, Saddam Hussein, because of Hussein's secular government policies and because of his

A Panamanian tanker burns in the Persian gulf after being attacked by Iraqi warplanes in April 1984.

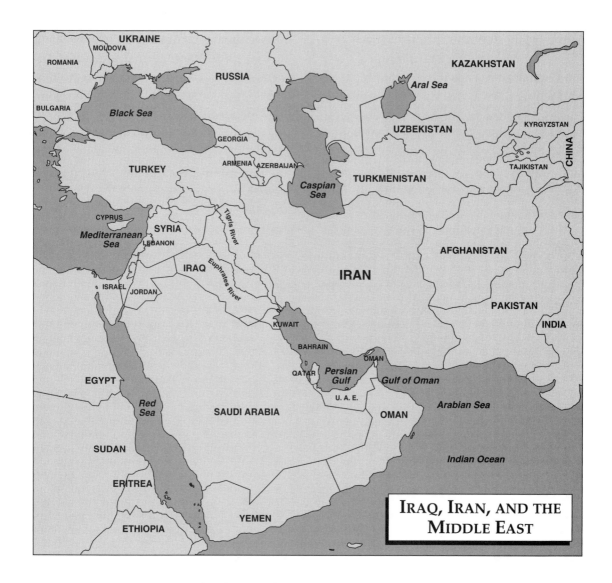

IRAQ, IRAN, AND THE
MIDDLE EAST

repressive actions against fundamentalist Muslims in Iraq. For his part, Hussein had come to dislike Khomeini for his encouragement of militant Muslim activists in Iraq. Both Khomeini and Hussein were shrewd and ambitious, and both sought to make their own nation the dominant power in the Persian Gulf region. This high-level clash of personal interests between Hussein and Khomeini compounded terri-

torial, cultural, and ethnic disputes that had long existed between Iran and Iraq.

FAR-REACHING REPERCUSSIONS

When the Iran-Iraq War broke out in 1980, few in the world saw the broader implications of the conflict. Both Khomeini and Hussein had alienated a great many members of the international community, and there was little concern among other nations over the fate of either Iran or Iraq. However, as the violence and devastation of the war intensified, the rest of the world gradually came to understand that the effects of the conflict were impacting more than just these two nations. As the war progressed, its potential for drawing in other nations, including the world's superpowers, became increasingly clear. The rest of the world eventually realized that war in the strategically vital Persian Gulf region was something they could not easily dismiss or minimize.

There was a long history of other nations involving themselves in the Persian Gulf region and the Middle East in general. However, the Iran-Iraq War marked a fundamental shift in the way foreign powers related to the nations in that area. Bernard Lewis, an author and Middle East historian, describes this change: "Outside powers no longer determined or directed the course of events in the Middle East, but the policies and actions of Middle Eastern governments provoked or invoked the intervention of . . . outside powers."[2] The world's most powerful nations would need to adjust to this new reality.

1 Conflict Evolves and Emerges

Conflict between Iraq and Iran was not new. For centuries and even millennia, peoples living in the region had clashed at various times over territory and over differences rooted in ethnicity and religion. Borders, particularly in southern Iraq and in critical strategic locations near the Persian Gulf itself, were disputed. The people of Iran (until 1935 known as Persia) were primarily of Indo-European origin, whereas most of the inhabitants of what is now Iraq were Arabs. And although the peoples of both Persia and Iraq were primarily Muslim, different forms of Islam—Shia in Persia and Sunni in Iraq—had long held sway in leading their respective nations. This division heightened the territorial and cultural tensions already existing between Persia and Iraq. Armed conflicts broke out periodically, and by the late twentieth century a general state of hostility had existed between the two nations for centuries.

CENTURIES OF CONFRONTATION

A critical point in the history of relations between Iran and Iraq was the Battle of Kadisiya in 637. At that time the new religion of Islam had been widely adopted by the Arabs, and they were spreading their new faith to much of the rest of the region through warfare and conquest. It was at Kadisiya that Arab armies defeated the Persians, who were at that time predominantly Zoroastrian. The battle is vividly described by Middle Eastern journalist Sandra Mackey in her book *The Iranians:*

> The heavily armed [Persian] cavalry with its supporting elephants . . . proved powerless against the Arabs on swift camels who attacked and then withdrew into the desert. Over three days, the two sides engaged. On the fourth, the Persians' . . . commander, Rustam, died. His army went into pell-mell retreat, leaving the [Persian] empire open to invasion.[3]

In this way, Persia came under Arab control and the strong influence of Islam. Persia subsequently underwent a series of conquests by outside powers before reemerging as independent in the early sixteenth century. Yet through all the turmoil, Persia remained Muslim. In the early seventeenth century, the ruling dynasty of Persia, the Safavids, adopted the

THE SUNNI-SHIA ISLAMIC SCHISM

All Muslims adhere to a belief stated in what is called the *shahada*, which claims that "There is no God but God, and Muhammad is the Messenger of God." However, members of the Shia branch of Islam add this to the *shahada*: "And Ali is the Friend of God." This puts the Shia branch in disagreement with the Sunni branch of Islam, the one to which most Muslims belong, over whom they consider worthy of being an Islamic spiritual leader.

The Shia believe Muhammad designated his cousin, Ali ibn Abi Talib, to be his successor as the leader of Islam. They claim that during a pilgrimage with a group of followers and family members at a place called Ghadir Khumm, Muhammad told the crowd, "For all those over whom I am master, Ali is also master. Oh God! Support all who support Ali and oppose all who oppose him."

After Muhammad's death, a power struggle developed over who should succeed him; most Muslim leaders supported another man, Abu Bakr, with whom they had a close relationship. Those who believed that Ali should succeed Muhammad and those who accepted Abu Bakr as leader evolved into today's Sunni and Shia Islam branches. The Shia maintain that Islamic spiritual leaders must be descended from Muhammad, while the Sunni do not require this.

Shia branch of Islam as Persia's official religion. Henceforward, Persia would be dominated both culturally and politically by Shiites.

Persia's adoption of Shia as its official religion contributed greatly to the tension between it and the Ottoman Empire that was then ruling Iraq. The Ottomans were Sunni Muslims, and although they agreed with the Shia on the basic tenets of Islam, they disagreed over whom they considered to be worthy to hold positions of religious leadership.

The Shia believed only descendants of Muhammad could act as Islamic leaders, while the Sunni believed any devout Muslim, regardless of heritage, could be a religious leader. The tensions lay in the fact that many sites sacred to the Shia lay within Ottoman territory. After years of conflict over access to these sites, the two sides came to terms regarding territorial boundaries in the area and free and safe passage for Persian Shia Muslims wishing to make pilgrimages to their holy shrines.

The founder of the Pahlavi dynasty, Reza Shah Pahlavi (1877–1944), stirred internal conflict with his policies of modernization and the breaking of long established cultural traditions.

Conflict reemerged in the nineteenth century, when nomadic Arab tribes who lived in the southern border area between Persia and Iraq became unhappy under Ottoman rule. Some of these tribes loosely allied themselves with Persia, and in 1812 they proclaimed their territory an autonomous state that they called Mohammera. This led to war in 1821, as the Persians and Ottomans both claimed rights to the territory of Mohammera. This dispute simmered for decades, but in 1913 a settlement was reached, helped greatly by intervention from Britain and Russia. These two powerful nations had involved themselves in the region in order to protect vital interests they had in maintaining access to the abundant mineral, oil, and natural gas resources found there. A meeting in Constantinople (later renamed Istanbul), Turkey, in 1913 led to the formation of a group, consisting of representatives from the Ottoman Empire, Persia, Britain, and Russia, to resolve conflicts. Britain and Russia were given superceding arbitrary powers, meaning they had the right to impose settlements in any subsequent conflicts.

MODERN IRAN AND IRAQ EMERGE

For Iraq, foreign domination of the sort exercised by Britain and Russia would continue well into the twentieth century. When the Ottoman Empire collapsed in 1918 after being defeated in World War I, by international agreement the British were given the task of overseeing the formation of many of the modern nation-states that had previously been Ottoman territories, including Iraq. At the same time, Persia came under the leadership of Reza Shah Pahlavi, who sought to modernize his nation and build its economic and military strength even as he worked to keep foreign interference in his nation's affairs to a minimum. Journalist and author Robin Wright, who has written extensively on Iran, describes Pahlavi as having "great ambitions," but also stirring internal conflict within Iran by seeking to "modernize ancient Persia by breaking the hold of tradition . . . that he believed prevented progress."[4] Pahlavi succeeded in modernizing and strengthening Iran, but he also angered and alienated Iranians who held traditional values and cultural preferences. This stirred debate and disagreement among Iranians over what was the best course for their country to take and whether Pahlavi's ideas and policies were in the nation's best interest.

Pahlavi antagonized Iraq by ending what was left of the autonomy of Mohammera, which he asserted was part of Iran itself, and which he renamed Khuzestan. Under Ottoman rule, Arabs had often received unfair treatment, and so Mohammera, in spite of being culturally Arabic, had generally allied itself with Persia. But now that Iraq was an independent Arab nation, Mohammera gravitated more naturally toward that country than toward Iran. At the same time, Iran suspected that Iraq was stirring up rebellion in the area.

Other territorial disputes roiled relations between the two nations. For exam-ple, Iraq contested existing agreements that had set the southern border between the two nations as the center of the Shatt al Arab, a river that connects the confluence of the Euphrates and Tigris Rivers with the Persian Gulf. Iraq now claimed territorial rights over the entire Shatt al Arab. Such a claim was bound to be provocative, since the Shatt al Arab provided critical access to the Persian Gulf for some otherwise landlocked areas of both nations.

With the outbreak of World War II, disputes between Iraq and Iran were pushed into the background. Various powers, notably Britain, the United States, and the Soviet Union, occupied both nations, using them as staging areas for supplying the Soviets, who were under siege from Nazi Germany. When foreign occupying forces withdrew after the war, it appeared that the new global alliances and international relationships that were developing might work to overcome the deep historical divisions between Iran and Iraq. Immediately after the war, both nations became part of a new Western strategy for countering Soviet communist expansion, and it appeared that lasting peaceful relations between them was possible.

Dilip Hiro, the author of several books on the Persian Gulf and Middle East, describes this period as "a generation of fairly peaceful co-existence between the two countries."[5] Iran and Iraq entered into an agreement called the Treaty of Good Neighborly Relations that led to ambassadorial relations between them. They also entered into a regional military alliance, along with Turkey, Pakistan, and Britain, called the Middle East Treaty Organization.

But while the 1950s began optimistically, two events took place later in that decade that contributed to instability in the area and, ultimately, to the outbreak of war between the two nations.

THE SEEDS OF TURBULENCE

The first event occurred in August 1953 in Iran, when Shah Muhammad Reza Pahlavi, the son and successor to Reza Shah Pahlavi, was restored to power by outside powers, especially the United States, after having been briefly overthrown in a coup led by a fervent nationalist named Muhammad Mosaddeq. Mosaddeq was the leader of the Iranian parliament, the Majlis, and he, like many members of the popularly elected body, opposed Pahlavi's policy of granting foreign powers control of Iran's oil industry. After more than two years of conflict with Mosaddeq and his followers, the Shah was forced to flee the country in fear of his life. His absence, however, lasted only four days.

After being restored to power, Pahlavi took a series of forceful actions to weaken the popularly elected Majlis and the nationalist movement among the populace. Continuing to enjoy Western support, Pahlavi became increasingly authoritarian. In return for this help, the Shah was decidedly pro-Western in his policies and positions. But there was great discontent among Iranians seeking greater independence from foreign influence, and there were long-term consequences for both the West and Pahlavi stemming from this partnership. Author Sandra Mackey says, "In

this mutually beneficial alliance . . . both the Shah and [Westerners] ignored the . . . threat to Iran's values and cultural identity posed by [the Shah's] reach for absolute power."[6]

The other event that destabilized relations between the two nations was a coup in 1958 staged by Iraqi military officers opposed to their nation's pro-Western monarchy. A nationalist republican, Abdul Karim Kassem, took control of Iraq. The new Iraqi leadership broke sharply from the previous government's pro-Western positions. Kassem withdrew from the Middle East Treaty Organization and adopted nonaligned (that is, not allied with Western powers or the Soviet Union) policies. Strident opposition to foreign influence in the region became one of the hallmarks of the new Iraqi regime.

DIVERGENT ONCE AGAIN

As the policies of the two nations toward the West diverged, so did their fortunes. Aided by experts from Britain and the United States, Iran's oil industry developed and expanded, and revenues from oil approximately quadrupled during the two decades after the Shah's restoration to power. Money was available to develop the nation's transportation, communication, and industrial infrastructure. Iran's educational system was reformed and improved, and Iran's literacy rate greatly increased. Meanwhile, land reform programs enabled some poor people to improve their standard of living. With money available to pay soldiers and arms

In 1951 Muhammed Mosaddeq led members of Iran's parliament in opposing Pahlavi's policy of allowing foreign powers to control the nation's oil industry.

purchased from the West, the Shah was able to build a military that was among the largest and most modern in the region. According to one description, Pahlavi used this wealth to "create his version of the modern Persian empire" and could fairly claim to be making progress toward "establishing Iran once again among the elite of nations."[7]

Iraq's economy and military experienced a fate dramatically different from Iran's. Between 1958 and 1968, Iraq under-went three different revolutions. Internal conflict among political and ethnic factions plagued each succeeding government, and the extreme political and social instability in Iraq severely hampered the country's economic development. Iraq's withdrawal from its treaties with other countries meant that the nation enjoyed none of the economic support or access to weapons that Shah Pahlavi's Iran had. Although Iraq, like its neighbor, possessed vast oil reserves, internal turmoil and economic

Kurdish rebels stand at the entrance to a cave used for shelter during their fight for independence from Iraq.

isolation prevented it from exploiting those resources fully. Because Iraq's rulers generally advocated socialist economic policies, the nation received some support from the communist Soviet Union. However, Iraq was not communist, and so never received the level of support the Soviets gave to communist client states. With so little international support, it was hardly surprising that Iraq was substantially weaker economically and militarily than Iran was during this period.

TERRITORIAL CONFLICTS REEMERGE

The two nations' divergent fortunes coincided with renewed territorial disputes. The international border had been designated as the median line of the deepest channel in the Shatt al Arab waterway, but in 1959 Iran moved to have the median line throughout the waterway recognized as the border, effectively expanding Iran's territory at Iraq's expense. Iraq refused the request, and attempts by the two nations to negotiate the dispute failed over the next ten years. Iran finally unilaterally withdrew from all agreements regarding its border with Iraq and began sending ships through the Shatt al Arab under armed escort and without regard to the national border. Iraq protested to the United Nations (UN), and some armed skirmishes occurred during the early 1970s, although Iran's vastly superior military was easily able to repel Iraq's attacks.

THE SHATT AL ARAB

"The frontier line in the Shatt-al-Arab shall follow the thalweg, i.e., the median line of the main navigable channel at the lowest navigable level, starting at the point from which the land frontier between Iran and Iraq enters the Shatt-al-Arab and continuing to the sea."

These words from the 1975 Algiers Accord set the border between Iran and Iraq through the Shatt al Arab to where it currently stands. The location of the international border within the Shatt al Arab had been a point of contention between Iran and Iraq for centuries. It was important to both nations that they be able to transport large cargo ships from their inland ports through the Shatt al Arab into the Persian Gulf. This meant having access to the parts of the river that were deep enough and wide enough to allow for passage of large cargo ships.

Modern design and technological progress have enabled cargo ships to be built with lower clearances, and other modes of transportation besides shipping have become increasingly common in modern times. Iran has also moved much of its oil industry to areas more directly accessible to the Persian Gulf. These changes have made previous territorial disputes over the Shatt al Arab largely irrelevant. Writing in the journal *Asian Affairs* in June 1986, Christopher Rundle, a British government foreign affairs expert, predicted during the Iran-Iraq War that "The Shatt-Al-Arab . . . will be less important after the war, precisely because neither Iran nor Iraq is likely to risk putting too many eggs in that basket."

Indeed, while Iran and Iraq continue to have disagreements and mostly unfriendly relations with each other, the border within the Shatt al Arab is no longer a point of contention. Some observers believe that even at the start of the Iran-Iraq War, the dividing line in the Shatt al Arab was no longer of real strategic significance and that Saddam Hussein, in citing access to the Shatt al Arab as a reason for going to war with Iran, was merely using it as a pretext.

For its part, Iraq renewed its objections to Iranian control of Khuzestan, claiming the area should be renamed Arabistan because of its large Arab population. Iraq also announced it was forming a group, the Popular Front for the Liberation of Arabistan, to fight against Iranian control of the area. In response, Iran began providing support for ethnic minorities within Iraq that were seeking independence and dissidents fighting against the national government's repression.

Now tensions between the two nations escalated to the point where war seemed likely. Iran claimed three islands in the Persian Gulf that had previously been occupied by the British but were inhabited and claimed by local Arab rulers. Iraq regarded this as an intrusion into Arab territory. In order to strengthen itself, Iraq signed a friendship treaty with the Soviet Union in 1972. This caused great concern not just on the part of the Iranian government, but also among its Western allies, who feared any Soviet presence in the region.

Countering Iraq's move to ally itself with the Soviets, Iran, with the support of the United States, provided extensive military support to one particular rebellious ethnic group, the Kurds. For centuries the Kurds had sought to establish their own nation in territories lying in northern Iraq, eastern Turkey, and northwestern Iran. Because of their strength and dominance in the north of Iraq, the Kurds presented an especially strong challenge to the country's unity. With the direct help of Iran and the indirect help of Western powers, Iraq's Kurds escalated their campaign for independence to a full-scale war against the government in Baghdad. As a result of this assistance, which even involved Iran sending two army regiments into Iraq, Kurdish forces succeeded in controlling significant chunks of territory.

Both Iran and Iraq had reason to exercise restraint in dealing with one another. For one thing Kurdish independence from Iraq also presented problems for Iran, as its own Kurdish minority could well be emboldened to seek independence themselves. Beyond this, both Iran and Iraq understood that their economies depended upon oil exports, so neither wanted to risk the certain damage that would come to their oil production capacity in a major war. With so much at stake, the two governments sought a third party to mediate their dispute. Secret negotiations began in 1975 under the auspices of Algeria, and in March, Iran and Iraq came to terms in an agreement known as the Algiers Accord.

THE ALGIERS ACCORD

The major provision of the Algiers Accord was the territorial division of the Shatt al Arab on the terms sought by Iran. In return for this concession, Iran agreed to stop supporting the Kurdish uprising in Iraq, and also closed its border to Kurdish rebels who had previously found refuge in Iran. Algerian president Houari Boumedienne, who negotiated the agreement, said that it "completely eliminated the conflict between the two brotherly countries."[8]

Iran honored its promise to end its support for the Kurds in Iraq, but other dissident groups within each country also lost support as a result of the Algiers Accord.

Among these were sizeable groups of Shia Muslim activists in both Iran and Iraq who opposed the largely secular policies of their respective governments. In Iraq, a group known as Al Daawa vehemently opposed the rule of the Baath Socialist Party, which had taken control of the country in 1968. Al Daawa engaged in and encouraged demonstrations and, in some cases, armed resistance. Likewise, in Iran, an elite group of Shia clergy known as the ulama opposed Pahlavi's regime. Although Iraq did not

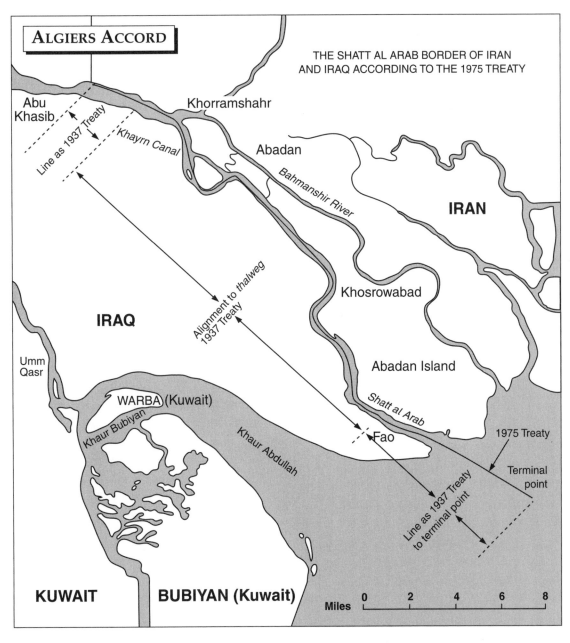

ALGIERS ACCORD

THE SHATT AL ARAB BORDER OF IRAN AND IRAQ ACCORDING TO THE 1975 TREATY

Abu Khasib

Khorramshahr

Line as 1937 Treaty

Khayrn Canal

Abadan

Bahmanshir River

IRAN

Alignment to *thalweg* 1937 Treaty

Khosrowabad

IRAQ

Abadan Island

Umm Qasr

Shatt al Arab

WARBA (Kuwait)

Fao

1975 Treaty

Khaur Bubiyan

Khaur Abdullah

Terminal point

Line as 1937 Treaty to terminal point

KUWAIT

BUBIYAN (Kuwait)

Miles   0   2   4   6   8

support the ulama directly, it nevertheless provided safe haven for its members and for others who opposed the Shah on religious grounds. Many of these exiles engaged in efforts to depose the Shah's government from the safety of Iraqi soil.

Iran urged Iraq to expel those within its territory who were stirring unrest, in line with the commitment made by both countries in the Algiers Accord to refrain from helping dissidents in the other. One Iranian who had taken up residence in Iraq to escape persecution from the Shah was unknown to most people in the world when, following his expulsion from Iraq, he resettled near Paris, France, in 1978. Though obscure, that person, Ayatollah Ruhollah Khomeini, was destined to become one of the most widely recognized and influential figures in the world.

AYATOLLAH KHOMEINI'S RISE TO PROMINENCE

Khomeini had long advocated government for Iran based upon Islamic principles. Khomeini also adamantly opposed the foreign influence in Iran that the Shah actively encouraged, believing that it corrupted Iranian culture. After speaking out exceptionally harshly against the Shah's rule, Khomeini had been exiled from Iran in November 1964. In one rabidly anti-Shah speech Khomeini had referred to the Shah as a "miserable wretch," and said: "The Shah is saying that he is granting liberty to the people.

Hear me, you pompous toad! Who are you to grant freedom? It is Allah who grants freedom, it is Islam which grants freedom."[9]

After being exiled from Iran, Khomeini lived for a time in Turkey before settling in Najaf, Iraq, where he continued to foment opposition to Pahlavi's rule and Iran's pro-Western, secularist policies. His printed writings and recorded speeches, smuggled into Iran and widely distributed, gained Khomeini many additional followers. Pahlavi therefore had good reason to consider Iraq's providing safe haven for Khomeini as a form of assistance to internal opposition.

Khomeini's expulsion from Iraq in 1978 at the Shah's request did not prevent him from spreading his message, however. France had especially strong communication and transportation links with Iran. Khomeini's followers were easily able to meet and correspond with him. In spite of the Shah's best efforts to muzzle him, Khomeini gained an increasingly large and dedicated following. In her book *The Iranians*, Mackey claims that actually, "Khomeini's influence grew precisely because he lived in exile. . . . Khomeini, able to pour his venom and wrath on the Shah from his sanctuary . . . became the champion of 'justice,' the single most important concept in Iranian political culture."[10]

THE ISLAMIC REVOLUTION IN IRAN

In spite of Khomeini's incessant efforts to drive him from power, Pahlavi managed

AYATOLLAH KHOMEINI, LIFETIME REVOLUTIONARY

When he led the 1979 revolution in Iran, Ayatollah Ruhollah Khomeini became, at seventy-six, the oldest person ever to lead a successful national revolution. Yet the lifetime experiences that would bring him that distinction began in the very earliest days of Khomeini's life.

Khomeini was born in the village of Khomein (from which he took his name) in southwestern Iran in 1902. Although he became orphaned at age sixteen (his father died before he turned one), Khomeini benefited from a prominent distinction: His family claimed direct descent from the Prophet Muhammad, the founder of the Islamic religion. This is especially important for Shia Muslims, who believe only a descendant of Muhammad can claim Islamic leadership. Khomeini therefore received religious instruction starting at a very early age. He came to revere the Islamic faith as an authoritative and guiding force.

After the deaths of both his parents, Khomeini studied under a prominent instructor named Abd al-Karim Ha'eri. These studies led him to Qom, considered one of Iran's holiest cities. Khomeini emerged as an outstanding student at Qom's *madreseh* (Islamic religious school). He graduated from the school and became a teacher there himself. In this role he gained the affection of students as well as the attention of religious leaders throughout the country. In 1961 he gained the title of ayatollah, the highest rank bestowed upon an Islamic cleric.

Khomeini distinguished himself from many of his colleagues by asserting that Muslim leaders and devout followers were obligated to fight against injustice and suffering everywhere. According to Khomeini, Islam prescribed principles for government and society as well as religion. As the best-informed people regarding Islamic teachings, the highest-ranking clergy were the best qualified to make important governing decisions. Over the course of many years, Khomeini wrote and spoke about his ideas on government based on Islamic religious principals. These beliefs and teachings were to become the basis for the fundamentalist Islamic government Khomeini would set up in Iran following the revolution.

to remain in control in Iran, largely because the Iranian people credited his policies for the good economic conditions the nation enjoyed. However, in the late 1970s a worldwide recession lessened demand for oil, Iran's most important export. Since much of the Iranian standard of living depended upon oil revenues, many Iranians who had generally supported the Shah suffered serious economic hardship and turned against him as a result. As his popular support waned, the Shah turned increasingly to his secret police, SAVAK, to suppress dis-

As Shah, Muhammad Reza Pahlavi continued his father's efforts to modernize Iran, but his authoritarian policies aroused widespread unrest.

sent. However, suspicions that the Shah's secret police had been responsible for the persecution of political opponents only caused further discontent.

Demonstrations against the Shah were met by still more repression by the government, and a cycle of violence set in that neither side seemed able to control. When an article in a government-controlled publication attacked Khomeini in January 1978, more demonstrations broke out, resulting in widespread death and injury. By this time, a combination of dissatisfaction with the Shah and his policies had created an opposition movement that was diverse and powerful. This broad-based anti-Shah sentiment was described in an article in *Time* magazine:

> Westernized intellectuals were infuriated by rampant corruption and repression; workers and peasants by the selective prosperity that raised glittering apartments for the rich while the poor remained in mud hovels; bazaar merchants by the Shah-supported businessmen who monopolized [money and supplies]; the clergy and their pious Muslim followers by the gambling casinos, bars and discotheques that seemed the most visible result of Westernization. Almost everybody hated the police terror.[11]

The protests against the Iranian monarch swelled until finally, on January 16, 1979, Shah Muhammad Pahlavi fled Iran for good. A temporary government took control, headed by prime minister Shahpour Bakhtiar. Bakhtiar had been an opponent of the Shah's, but in a last desperate effort to save his regime, Pahlavi had made some concessions to the opposition, one of which had been appointing Bakhtiar as prime minister. Now that those efforts had failed, Bakhtiar offered to work with Khomeini on forming a new national leadership. But Khomeini rejected any compromise with this Shah-appointed government, claiming it was illegal and saying he would arrest the people in the government and "appoint a government with the support of the Iranian people."[12] That Khomeini might have a strong enough following to deliver on that claim was shown by the demonstration that turned out to greet him upon his return to Iran. Wright describes the scene:

> Despite the bitter cold, public outpourings of support were rapturous from the moment [Khomeini's plane] was first sighted. . . . Tehran echoed with . . . cheering and car honking in long and repetitive bursts. . . .
>
> As Khomeini's motorcade inched along a twenty-mile route through the capital, many men and women sobbed openly, the joy mixed with disbelief. Above the din, street vendors loudly hawked Khomeini pennants, portraits and pins. Despite the deployment of fifty thousand volunteer marshalls . . . Iranians mobbed the convoy. Hundreds ran alongside until they dropped from exhaustion. Even conservative estimates numbered the crowd at no less than three million. Iranians wanted change, and the Ayatollah's return marked the moment for catharsis.[13]

On February 1, 1979 Ayatollah Khomeini returned to Iran after fifteen years in exile. The Shah's appointed government resigned a few days later.

In the face of massive demonstrations in favor of Khomeini, Bakhtiar and the other members of his caretaker government resigned. The fate of Iran would now be in the hands of Khomeini and his followers. Their avid devotion to fundamentalist Islamic principals and Iranian independence would bear heavily upon the future governance of the nation, including its relations with neighboring Iraq.

Chapter

2 Militants Take Power: War Breaks Out

Khomeini had demonstrated himself to be determined, politically astute, and charismatic in leading the Islamic Revolution in Iran. In confronting Iraq, however, Khomeini was to come up against Saddam Hussein, who likewise was a formidable leader, but whose vision for his nation was very different. Some observers have claimed the Iran-Iraq War was as much a personal clash between two forceful and charismatic national leaders as it was between the nations themselves. Robin Wright elaborates:

> Khomeini . . . was the oldest leader in the Middle East. His dream was the revival of Islam to replace the . . . modern ideologies of capitalism and communism—especially in countries, such as Iraq, where injustice reigned. To the ayatollah, the Iraqi Shi'a were the victims of [Baath] rule. Although the Shi'a constituted the majority, they were generally excluded from the political system and their incomes and standards of living were generally the lowest. . . . Khomeini's vendetta . . . was also personal. Baghdad's expulsion of the ayatollah in 1978 had been ordered by then vice president Saddam Hussein;

Khomeini never forgave Saddam for selling out to the Shah.[14]

However, Hussein had ambitions of his own that directly clashed with Khomeini's objectives:

> At forty-three, [Hussein] . . . was then one of the two youngest heads of state in the Middle East. His pan-Arab socialism was avowedly secular, and his agenda was to modernize Iraq, particularly its military. . . . [Hussein] aspired to become the new regional leader. . . . The main obstacle was Iran's zealous Islamic ideology.[15]

IRAN'S RADICAL NEW COURSE

Khomeini lost no time cutting Iran's ties to the West, and, due to his inflammatory statements about nations that had supported the Shah, he quickly became regarded by the West as a rogue leader. He was on record, for example, as saying, "All Western governments are just thieves, nothing but evil comes from them."[16] The United States in particular was associated, along with the Shah, with evil and with

Satan. With Iran's new leader directing such harsh statements at many of the world's major powers, observers easily overlooked other statements that expressed the same level of hatred toward Iran's smaller and historically weaker neighbor, Iraq.

Khomeini, however, made no secret of the contempt he felt for Saddam Hussein.

He had previously named Hussein and his Iraqi Baath government as an enemy of Iran on a par with the Shah and the United States. In a statement that reflected both his personal dislike for the Iraqi leader and the long-standing ethnic and religious differences between Iran and Iraq, Khomeini also said of Hussein: "This deviated person is completely uninformed about Islam,

A crowd of Khomeini supporters kneel in prayer at Tehran University in February 1979.

and, among other things, is an Arab. God, the most high, said, the Arabs are very hard in infidelity and hyprocrisy."[17]

The Ayatollah's opposition to Hussein went beyond personal animus, however. To Khomeini, Iraq seemed the next likely place for the staging of an Islamic revolution. During the time of his exile in Iraq, Khomeini had witnessed the repressive and brutal treatment of his fellow militant Shiites by the Iraqis. Furthermore, he opposed Iraq's secularism just as much as he had Iran's.

However, before Khomeini could export his revolution, he had to consolidate his position at home. There were many in Iran who had opposed the Islamic Revolution, and even among those who had supported it as a means of ousting the Shah, not everyone agreed with Khomeini's fundamentalist religious views. To secure their position, therefore, the revolutionaries purged Iran's military and other government institutions to eliminate potential political opponents. Local members of the Revolutionary Council, made up mostly of radical clergy, engaged in repression and atrocities comparable to that which had taken place under the Shah. Strict codes concerning dress and behavior were imposed on the nation, and members of the Revolutionary Council harassed and even attacked citizens who failed to comply. Especially brutal were ad hoc (improvised) tribunals that judged individuals suspected of vaguely defined counterrevolutionary activities—specifics were rarely provided during hearings. One judge who presided over these tribunals espoused the frightening view "that unsuitable individuals should be liquidated so others can live free."[18] Acting without any oversight, these tribunals carried out trials, sentencing, and punishments, including many brutal executions.

The harshness with which any opponents were treated cost the new government much of the goodwill and support it had previously enjoyed among Iranians. What would prove to be of greater consequence to the new government, however, were its purges of high-ranking, experienced military officers suspected of being loyal to the Shah. These officers had the training and military know-how to make them a threat to the new regime, but their removal would prove severely damaging to the nation's security.

A War of Words and Subversion

In the midst of this internal turmoil, Khomeini clung to his determination to export fundamentalist Islamic revolution to Iraq. He provided arms and support to militant Shia Muslims in Iraq and allowed them to take refuge in Iran. He also resumed aid to the Iraqi Kurds, and frequently spoke out against the Iraqi leadership, urging the people to rise up and overthrow their secular government as Iranians had done.

Relations between the two nations deteriorated further in April 1980, when the Iraqi militant fundamentalist group Al Daawa, with apparent Iranian support, attempted to assassinate a group of Iraqi officials. The Iraqi government responded by

Iraqi Shiites carry an empty coffin through the streets of Damascus, Syria, to protest the execution of a prominent Iraqi cleric, Ayatollah Sadr.

executing a prominent Shia cleric, Ayatollah Sadr, along with his sister, who was also prominent among the Iraqi Shia. The attempted assassinations and subsequent executions raised the anger and bitterness on both sides to potentially explosive levels and set off a series of escalating actions and counteractions. Gary Sick, a one-time U.S. National Security Council official, would later comment that "the events of April 1980 represented the crucial turning point that eventually led to war."[19]

When he learned about the executions of Sadr and his sister, Khomeini vented his fury by calling upon Iraq's army to take action against the government and the Baath Party that was leading Iraq. "As the Iranian army joined their people [in their struggle against the Shah]," said Khomeini, "oh Iraqi army, join your people. . . . The people and army of Iraq must turn their backs on the Baath regime and overthrow it . . . because this regime is attacking Iran, attacking Islam and the [Koran]."[20]

THE RISE OF SADDAM HUSSEIN

The most prominent target of Khomeini's wrath, Saddam Hussein, had already proven that he would be a worthy opponent. Hussein's political career had begun at age eighteen when he went to Iraq's largest city and capital, Baghdad, and joined the Baath Socialist Party. The Baaths supported unification of Arab peoples and socialist economic policies, and

SADDAM HUSSEIN'S MILITANT UPBRINGING

The influences that shaped Saddam Hussein as a national leader began at an early age. Hussein's father, Hussein al-Majid, died even before his son was born in April of 1937 outside the northern Iraqi city of Tikrit. Hussein was raised by a maternal uncle, Khairallah Talfah. Talfah supported a nationalistic government movement that opposed Western intervention in Iraq. His political activities got him kicked out of the Iraqi military during World War II, as well as a five-year prison sentence. In *Saddam Hussein: A Political Biography*, Efraim Karsh and Inari Rautsi say: "These events had a profound effect on Saddam's life. . . . his empathy with [Talfah] had a crucial impact on the development of his nationalist sentiments in that it fueled a deep-seated hatred of [the Iraqi] monarchy and the foreign power behind it, a feeling which he was to harbor for years to come."

When Hussein left Tikrit for Baghdad, the influence his uncle had had upon him was a primary factor in motivating Hussein to join the Iraqi Baath Socialist Party. As a party member Hussein was even further steeped in Arab nationalism and militant opposition to foreign domination of Iraq. These influences upon a young Saddam Hussein would prove to have an enormous long-term impact both upon the nation of Iraq and the entire world when Hussein came to power.

they opposed the pro-Western monarchy ruling Iraq at that time. After the 1958 revolution, Hussein was injured fighting for the Baaths against Kassem's government forces. He fled the country, returning in 1963 after a successful joint overthrow of Kassem by the military and Baath forces, but was forced later that same year to go underground after the Baath Party was purged from the new government by Iraq's leader, Abd al-Salam Arif. During this time Hussein rose in the party's ranks, becoming the assistant secretary general and the head of the party's militia. It was while he was in exile and underground in Iraq that Hussein acquired the cunning, ruthlessness, and opportunistic characteristics that he would come to be known for as Iraq's leader.

Hussein was only thirty-one when the Baaths seized power in 1968. Though not a member of the inner circle of party leadership, Hussein benefited from a reputation for effectiveness he had earned during the years of struggle, and also from the fact that the new Baath ruler, Ahmad Hassan Bakr, was a kinsman. Once the Baaths were in control of Iraq,

Saddam Hussein's combination of cunning, ruthlessness, natural leadership ability, and charisma helped him seize control of the Iraqi government in 1979.

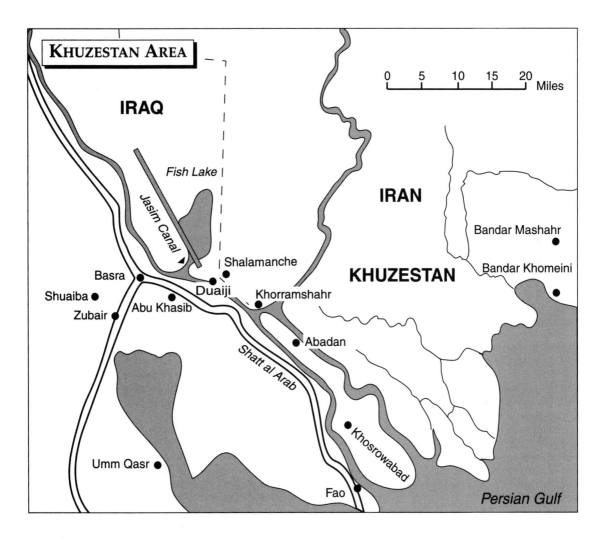

Hussein helped consolidate their power and at the same time elevated himself within the new government by overseeing the restructuring of the nation's military and bureaucracy and the installation of loyalists in leading roles within these institutions. Hussein was also responsible for thousands of arrests of political opponents, some of whom were subsequently tried and killed in televised executions. At the same time, Hussein worked to build support for the government among Iraq's masses by offering improved economic conditions and greater popular representation in government. By 1975 Hussein had risen to a position within the government of second in command, behind his kinsman. Yet Hussein's activism and cleverness enabled his true powers to exceed his position. Hiro describes the situation that developed:

> As a youthful, energetic figure, Saddam Hussein appealed to those Baathists who believed in strong ideology and

commitment to socio-economic progress. By the mid-1970s he had outstripped Bakr in leadership, cunning, ruthlessness, organizational ability and charisma. . . . He still needed Bakr, a former military officer with [a mild] personality whose moderation and piety went down well with the older, conservative segments of society.[21]

However, events would soon unfold that would enable Hussein to break with Bakr, remove him from power, and step up as the sole, supreme ruler of Iraq.

Although Hussein was well on his way to taking control in Iraq, Khomeini's heated rhetoric and threats understandably alarmed him. The Islamic Revolution in Iran was the most obvious example of what could result from rising Shia discontent and activism in the region. With the Shia actually representing a slight majority among the Muslims in Iraq as well, Iraqi government officials had good reason to be concerned about any encouragement of religious radicalism. Massive demonstrations among Iraqi Shiites in

KHOMEINI AND TWELVER SHIISM

Among the major subgroups that developed within the Shia branch of Islam, the Twelver Shia branch is the largest. Ayatollah Khomeini and his most devout followers were members of this group. Twelvers believe that after Muhammad, the next twelve leaders of Islam, known as imams, were all legitimate rulers. The last of these, Muhammad al-Mahdi, is said to have mysteriously disappeared, and therefore became known as the Hidden Imam. Twelvers believe that Mahdi will reappear someday, leading an army that destroys evil throughout the world, including oppressive governments, then rule for a thousand years of peace and justice.

Among those most enamored of Khomeini, some believed him to be the Hidden Imam, the one who had come to liberate them from evil and corruption. His success in overthrowing a government regarded as corrupt and oppressive by many Shia, and his heated rhetoric and militant actions against powerful nations, convinced some even more that he was indeed the vanished Mahdi. They hoped Khomeini was destined to fight and defeat righteous Islam's foes and rule over a world of peace and justice for the oppressed Islamic faithful.

Iraq premier El Bakr (second from left) was placed under house arrest and forced to resign when he refused to execute Iraqi military officers accused of disloyalty by Saddam Hussein.

June 1979 against the Baath regime validated that concern. Aware of the real threat the demonstrators posed to his ambitions, but also seeing an opportunity to exploit the situation, Hussein submitted to Bakr a list of dissidents he said should be executed. The list included military officers Hussein claimed had been secretly involved with the recent unrest. Bakr opposed executing military officers, but most Baath officials sided with Hussein, and Bakr was placed under house arrest and

later resigned, supposedly for health reasons. Hussein took over all of Bakr's official government positions. Some diplomats reportedly were surprised by this development, but historical author Trevor Mostyn notes, "The transfer of power had been meticulously planned by Hussein and was widely expected."[22]

When Hussein gained full and unchallenged control of Iraq, he took over a nation that was economically and militarily stronger than it had been at any time in recent memory. Still, since the time Iraq had become an independent nation, it had been weaker than Iran for various reasons. Iraq had a smaller population, less oil-production capacity, and fewer trading partners among large, wealthy nations. Iran also had more territory, and its much longer coastline afforded it greater access to the Persian Gulf and the Arabian Sea.

Another major disadvantage Iraq faced was internal divisions among its population. Over 60 percent of Iran's population was ethnic Persian, and over 90 percent was Shia Muslim. By contrast, although Iraq was over 70 percent Arab, the people were far less unified in their religion, being almost evenly divided between the Shia and Sunni branches. In addition, the Kurds also constituted about 20 percent of Iraq's population, a larger portion than any single ethnic minority in Iran. Furthermore, with the Shia concentrated in the southern part of the country and the Kurds in the north, Iraq faced serious regional divisions.

Saddam Hussein's answer to these divisions was to offer himself and the Baath Party as the linchpins for Iraqi unity. Middle East expert Charles Tripp, author of *A History of Iraq*, elaborates:

> Once he assumed the presidency, a personality cult of awesome proportions was created around Saddam Hussein. It portrayed him as the representative of all the peoples of Iraq, both in their particular identities as members of different communities, and in their common condition as subjects of the Iraqi government. National institutions were created to

sustain the national myths. The Baath Party was now a countrywide organization, reaching down to the smallest village and most modest neighborhood in an unprecedented way.[23]

In addition to sweeping purges of government organizations, Hussein promoted crackdowns on Shia dissidents as a means of strengthening his government's position, although these initiatives further antagonized Khomeini. In addition to Ayatollah Sadr and his sister, Hussein also ordered the executions of nearly one hundred civilian and military leaders in the spring of 1980. About half of those killed were Al Daawa members, and subsequently mere membership in Al Daawa became a crime punishable by death in Iraq.

Meanwhile, just as Khomeini had worked to stir discontent in Iraq, Hussein worked to foment unrest in Iran. In response to Khomeini's calls for his overthrow and his assistance to Iraqi Kurdish and Shia dissidents, Hussein provided assistance to Iranian Kurds who opposed their nation's government and to Arabs in Khuzestan seeking independence. In an additional gesture of hostility, Hussein expelled about sixteen thousand Iranian-born Iraqi residents. Finally, the Iraqi government also provided safe haven and assistance to former high-ranking members of the Iranian military who had been loyal to the Shah. These exiles were permitted to broadcast anti-Khomeini propaganda from radio stations within Iraq and to mount attempts to overthrow the revolutionary government of Iran during the first half of 1980.

THE FIRST FLARE-UPS

At the same time, there were dozens of minor border skirmishes between the two countries. Then armed hostilities escalated when, on September 2, Iranian and Iraqi troops exchanged heavy fire near the Iranian border town of Qasr-e Sharin. Iran responded by shelling and bombing two Iraqi towns, Khanaqin and Mandali, two days later. After Iraq stated it would capture the central border village Zain al Qaws, which it claimed Iran had ceded under terms of the Algiers Accord, Iran fired upon Iraqi border towns near that disputed village. Over the course of a week, Iraq captured this area, along with several other border posts. It appeared Iraq had undertaken an ambitious offensive, and on September 17, when Saddam Hussein made a televised speech before Iraq's national assembly, he left no doubt about his military intentions.

HUSSEIN RENOUNCES THE ALGIERS ACCORD

During his speech, Hussein dramatically tore up a copy of the Algiers Accord, saying that Iran had already violated the treaty by assisting dissident groups within Iraq. He also faulted Iran for not turning over territory it had ceded in the

Saddam Hussein addresses Iraqi troops in September 1980, prior to the invasion of Iran.

Algiers Accord in exchange for a favorable determination on the Shatt al Arab waterway. Throughout the speech, Hussein took a belligerent stance. He asserted that Iran was threatening not just Iraq, but the whole Arab world, and made it clear that Iraq was ready to go to war:

> We say before . . . the whole world that we unmasked the distorted pretext of the ruling clique in Iran, who employed the camouflage of religion to expand at the expense of Arab sovereignty, high Arab interests and to create unrest and division among the Arab people. And so [the Shatt al Arab], as it has always been through history, returns to be Iraqi and Arab, in name and truth, including all rights of full sovereignty. [Iraq] will act with strength and ability against anybody who may challenge this legitimate decision.[24]

Within a few days Iraq launched multiple waves of air raids against Iranian air force bases in advance of a massive ground invasion. This invasion took place on September 22, with Iraqi forces crossing the border along an eight-hundred-mile front. The Iraqis quickly captured a number of strategic positions: heights along the road linking Baghdad to Tehran, territory in Iranian Kurdistan that blocked Iranian forces' ability to move toward Iraq, and the town of Mehran in the south-central region, which put the Iraqis in the position to threaten several important Iranian military and oil-production sites.

During the following month, heavy fighting occurred around Khorramshahr, Iran's largest port, in the southern border area. The city fell to Iraqi troops on November 10, by which time the southern Iranian cities of Dezful, Ahvaz, and Abadan were also under heavy siege. Overall, by mid-November, Iraq occupied Iranian soil along about half their common border, with penetrations ranging from six to twenty-five miles deep.

Iran responded to the Iraqi incursions by using its superior naval forces to blockade the port city of Basra, Iraq's only major access point to the Persian Gulf. Iran's air force also staged effective strikes against Iraqi targets, particularly oil fields, pipelines, and refineries. As a result of these attacks, Iraq's oil exports were reduced to one-sixth their prewar level during the closing months of 1980.

On the ground, however, Iranian forces fared poorly. In January 1981, Iran launched a hastily planned counteroffensive in Khuzestan, but because the army units were inadequately trained and undermanned, the result was a devastating defeat for the Iranians. An attempt in February to expel Iraqi forces from Iranian Kurdistan was equally unsuccessful. These two campaigns were costly: Between them, Iran lost a total of nearly two hundred tanks. Although the Iraqis made no additional significant territorial gains, they did consolidate their initial gains and secure supply routes before the onset of winter, when heavy rains forced a pause in combat.

The opening phase of the war seemed to indicate that Iraq had gained an advantage over Iran. Iran's military remained larger than Iraq's, but internal instability following Iran's revolution and its subsequent alienation from its former allies

THE U.S.-IRAN HOSTAGE CRISIS

After a group of militant students overran the U.S. embassy and took the workers and residents hostage there in November 1979, the Iranian government expressed support for the students and made what it said were nonnegotiable demands in return for the hostages' release. These included the return of the Shah, who had been admitted into the United States for medical treatment, the return of Iranian assets the new Iranian government claimed the Shah had stolen, and a public apology from the U.S. government for its support of the Shah and Iranian policies during his reign.

The world was shocked over the events in Iran. No nation was prepared for the possibility that its foreign embassies would be attacked and its diplomats taken prisoner with the support of the host government, regardless of how strained the relationship between two nations might be. The disregard Iran showed for international opinion and accepted standards of diplomacy served to alienate it from most of the world, leaving it isolated and with few trading or military partners during the Iran-Iraq War.

After several failed attempts at negotiations and an attempted rescue of the hostages that ended in disaster for the military forces conducting the operation, the U.S. embassy hostages were finally released in January 1981, 444 days after the crisis began. By that time the Iran-Iraq War was underway, with Iraqi forces having invaded Iran.

An American hostage is paraded by his captors before cameras in November 1979.

seriously hindered Iran's ability to counter Iraq's aggression. Iran's ablest military leaders had been purged or exiled, and large numbers of rank-and-file soldiers had deserted. The severity of the manpower shortage was dramatized when the new army chief of staff stated, "I inherited an army that didn't have a single soldier in Tehran."[25]

The Iranian military was also plagued by an inability to obtain spare parts and replacement equipment, a result of Khomeini's vociferous anti-Western rhetoric having antagonized most of the nations that had previously supplied Iran's weapons. Iran's alienation from the rest of the world was particularly acute because of a prolonged crisis over the holding of several dozen diplomats as hostages by radicals who had stormed the U.S. embassy in Tehran in November of 1979. Khomeini had refused to intervene to force the release of the hostages and ultimately even announced that the embassy seizure was justified, claiming the U.S. government "had turned its so-called embassy into a base for espionage and conspiracy against Iran."[26] A tense standoff ensued that lasted over a year. In such a hostile climate, it was little wonder that the nations that were in the best position to assist Iran militarily would not consider doing so.

Internal division was also a hindrance to Iran's war effort. Among the Iranian civilian population there were numerous factions either not enthusiastic about Khomeini's Islamic government or outright opposed to it. Divisions between the militant clergy in the new regime and more pragmatic lay officials also worked against Iran. The greatest threat and cause of insta-

bility within Iran, however, was the presence of armed internal opposition, especially from a group known as the Mojahaddin-i-Khalq. This group, which combined Islam with leftist political and economic views, had supported Khomeini during the revolution but had felt excluded by him since he had come to power. In fact, a virtual civil war was underway between the government and the Mojahaddin that included bombings, shoot-outs, assassinations, and additional government repression aimed at suspected Mojahaddin members. By diverting attention and resources away from the war with Iraq, this internal conflict would seriously hamper Iran for the first four years of the war.

Meanwhile, Iraq was for the first time in some years able to reap the benefits of being a unified state with a strong central government. During the years leading up to the war, Iraq had greatly increased its international trade, particularly by exporting oil, and government coffers were flush with hard foreign currency. With money to spend, Iraq had been able to greatly strengthen its national economy; the Iraqi people, enjoying an increased standard of living, were largely supportive of their government. Most significantly for its war-making capability, Iraq had also been able to purchase the most modern weapons available and expand its military forces.

Uncertain Intentions

While Hussein had significant resources to draw upon at the start of the war, he only committed limited forces to the first offen-

Iraqi troops construct a bridge across the Euphrates River near Khorramshahr in October 1980.

sives against Iran, leaving some doubt as to just what his objectives were. Charles Tripp claims that Hussein "saw a limited war against Iran as a way of forcing the Iranian regime to acknowledge that the balance of power had shifted in favour of Iraq."[27] This acknowledgment, Tripp contends, was to take the form of the whole of the Shatt al Arab being recognized as belonging to Iraq.

Other experts on the Persian Gulf region have claimed that Hussein wanted only to lessen the threat of being overthrown by an exported Islamic revolution. The Iraqi deputy prime minister at the time, Tariq Aziz, who would later become foreign minister, claimed that his government wanted "neither to destroy Iran nor

to occupy it permanently because that country is a neighbor with which we will remain linked by geographical and historic bonds and common interests."[28]

Whatever his motives, most likely Hussein hoped for a short and limited war, but his early reluctance to risk substantial forces likely prevented him from reaping any quick and easy benefits from his attacks against Iran. According to Tripp, after the first few months of the war, "it was clear that the short, demonstrative war planned by Saddam Hussein had become something very different."[29] Indeed, the Iran-Iraq War would turn out to be a far longer and costlier conflict than Hussein— or anyone else for that matter—had likely expected.

3 Settling into Stalemate

With Saddam Hussein either unwilling or unable to devote the resources necessary to immediately overrun his adversary at the time when Iran was most vulnerable, the early Iraqi battlefield gains were short-lived. Within two years, Iran had reversed its early losses and put Iraq on the defensive. Yet during the first few years of the war, neither country was able to gain a significant breakthrough against the other. With both nations fully mobilized, the war developed into a protracted standoff.

IRANIAN RESURGENCE AND RETALIATION

In spite of Iraqi successes, there was a little good news for Iran during the opening phase of the war. Besides the damage inflicted on Iraq by Iranian air raids and the successful blockade of Basra, the result Iraq had hoped for in the Iranian province of Khuzestan had failed to materialize. This is summed up by international affairs author Geoff Simons in *Iraq: From Sumer to Saddam:* "Contrary to Saddam's expectations, the Arabs in Khuzistan/Arabistan did not rise up to greet their Arab liberators but [instead] fled in panic from the area."[30]

Furthermore, as the war progressed, it became clear that Iraq's initial success in its ground war had been much more attributable to Iranian weakness than to Iraqi military prowess. While Iraq possessed plenty of weapons and equipment and had large numbers of combat troops, most of those fighters were unskilled or inexperienced. Having laid siege to critical cities in Khuzestan, for example, they proved unable to complete the conquest of any but Khorramshahr.

Leadership was also a problem for the Iraqis. Tactical and strategic decisions came down from Saddam Hussein himself, not from field commanders and career military officers. Since Hussein lacked any real understanding of battlefield strategy or tactics, Iraq often overextended its forces or failed to capitalize on opportunities to capture additional ground.

Internal divisions also hampered Iraq. Calls by Khomeini for Shia Iraqis to turn against their own government were not heeded on a widespread basis, but with a large number of Shia conscripts among Iraq's forces, there were enough incidents of dissent, desertion, and even some armed attacks by militant Shiites in the armed forces against fellow fighters to cause concern among the government and military leadership.

On the other hand, while Iraq failed to make the most of its advantages, Iran rapidly corrected many of the weaknesses it displayed at the outset of hostilities. In expecting that Khomeini's relatively weak government would be unable to mount an effective response to his aggression, Hussein, it turned out, had miscalculated. In their book *Saddam Hussein: A Political Biography*, Efraim Karsh and Inari Rautsi, two experts on Middle Eastern affairs, comment on at least one factor Hussein likely failed to consider:

A revolutionary regime under attack is all the more likely to respond with vehemence when it has not yet gained full legitimacy and still has many internal enemies. History has shown that attacking a destabilized society in the throes of revolution tends to unify it, for the enemies within suddenly seem much less threatening than those without.[31]

In the case of Iran, many who had deserted from the military returned to their posts, and new volunteers and conscripts swelled the ranks of the armed forces even further as the threat posed by the Iraqi

Iraqi troops defend their position againt an Iranian counterattack.

Women members of the Iran's Revolutionary Guard participate in a rally in Tehran. The Revolutionary Guards were responsible for protecting the government from internal enemies and defending positions around Iranian cities and towns.

invasion became clear. Furthermore, tensions that had existed between the traditional military units and a pro-Khomeini militia called the Revolutionary Guards faded into the background. Following the revolution, there had existed a division of duties between these two forces that was decidedly unfair: The Revolutionary Guards usually assumed duties of guarding the government against internal enemies and taking up defensive positions around cities and towns, while the Iranian army undertook more dangerous direct combat roles.

However, after the seriousness of the Iraqi threat became clear, Iran's armed forces began to work together more closely. Military unity was also strengthened as Islamic hardliners became overwhelmingly dominant within Iran's government and installed more people into the military's command structure who shared their fervent Islamic beliefs and saw the conflict with Iraq as a sacred struggle.

The replacement of weapons and parts for military equipment was another serious problem that the Iranians were able to alleviate. Although many nations had ended trade within Iran, and the major military powers of the world remained largely unwilling to supply Khomeini's forces with arms, Iran was able to obtain many of the weapons and spare parts it needed from Vietnam, which had come into possession of a considerable supply when the United States hastily withdrew from that country in the mid-1970s. Iran also got help from other Muslim nations with hostile relations with the United States, such as Libya and Syria, and from North Korea and a few other countries. In the end, Iran was able to resupply its military without compromising its strident rhetoric against Western powers.

IRAN TURNS THE TABLES

Bolstered by new supplies and recruits, Iran scored its first major success on the ground in late September 1981, when two infantry divisions engaged the Iraqi troops surrounding the city of Abadan. After a week of fighting, the Iranians drove the invaders back to the west bank of the Karun River, a few miles away from the city. Other successes soon followed.

THE MA'DAN

The marshy areas in southern Iraq that were the target of Iran's Majnoon offensive are also home to an ethnic group of Iraqis known as the Ma'dan, or Marsh Arabs. Inaccessibility to these areas and a lack of communication with the nation's major cities has kept the Ma'dan largely isolated, and they have maintained most of their ancient customs and lifestyles. They make their homes on boats, rafts, and floating islands, creating large huts made entirely from reeds for dwellings. The Ma'dan rely mostly on hunting and fishing for food. Traditionally, the Ma'dan fish using a five-pronged spear. Floating villages include a guest house known as a *mudhif*, where any traveler adventurous enough to wander into the marshes is welcome to stay and be entertained by the village sheikh, or chief.

The Ma'dan originated in the ninth century when ex-slaves and outcasts rebelled against the ruling authorities and sought refuge in the marshes. Since then there have been recurring tensions between the Ma'dan and the governments in power in Iraq. The Ma'dan have maintained a low-level rebellion against the Hussein regime since the end of the war between Iraq and an international alliance in 1991.

Between November of that year and February 1982, Iran launched several smaller attacks against the Iraqi positions within its own borders, retaking additional territory in the southern sector near Abadan and also regaining ground in the areas of Susangard and Qasr-e Sharin. In March, Iran attacked on the eve of the Iranian New Year, *No Ruz*, catching the Iraqis by surprise. With commando units striking behind enemy lines and seven divisions attacking frontline positions, Iran inflicted heavy damage: As many as forty thousand Iraqis were killed, injured, or captured, and over six hundred tanks were captured or destroyed. Iran regained over nine hundred square miles of territory and pushed the invaders back to within a few miles of the border.

As the year went on, Iran continued to regain lost territory and inflict damage upon their enemy. In April and May, Iran

Jubilant Iranian soldiers celebrate after driving the Iraqis out of the Abadan area in February of 1982.

launched massive offensives in the areas of Dezful and Khorramshahr, using about seventy thousand troops and two hundred tanks. These forces succeeded in recapturing the strategic city of Khorramshahr by the end of May, along with substantial territory to the north and east. Together with their earlier counteroffensives the previous November, Iran had regained over three thousand square miles of territory, about a third of the total that had been taken by Iraq. Overall, this campaign effectively ended the sieges of key cities in Khuzestan.

These gains reflected the advantage Iran had in terms of its significantly larger population. Especially effective in these Iranian offensives was the tactic of human-wave attacks. These assaults consisted of massive numbers of people, usually only lightly armed, charging against hardened artillery positions. Wright describes the use of this tactic in one battle:

> Roughly a hundred thousand Iranian troops . . . were committed to Operation *Fath*. At 4:30 A.M. on March 22, they moved in six columns along a fifty-mile front in oil-rich southern Khuzistan. . . . Wave after wave of Iranian troops drove at the Iraqis, hoping to wear out the troops and use up their ammunition. After one column of [Iranians] dropped, it was followed by another group of frenzied troops, usually urged on by mullahs attached to each unit.[32]

Although Iraqi forces enjoyed great superiority in heavy armor and quantities of ammunition, Iran's human-wave attacks proved highly effective. Defenders would eventually use up ammunition and exhaust themselves trying to hold off the relentless onslaught of attackers. After the use of human-wave attacks proved effective in a battle in November 1981 that recaptured the southern Iranian city of Bostan, the tactic became a mainstay of Iran's war strategy.

Meanwhile, Iran's significantly larger land area also proved an advantage, at least early in the war. Iranian bombers were able to reach targets throughout Iraq, while many strategically important targets in Iran were out of the range of Iraqi warplanes. For example, in April 1981 Iranian warplanes responded to Iraqi missile attacks against Iranian troop concentrations by striking an Iraqi air base on Iraq's western border with Syria, a round-trip of over one thousand miles. Similarly, the Iranians responded to Iraqi shelling of Iran's largest oil refinery in Abadan by decimating most of Iraq's major oil refineries with large-scale air attacks.

At this stage of the war, air and missile attacks had little if any bearing on the ground war or on either side's overall strategy. However, Iran's ferocious response to Iraq's air and missile attacks did, for a while, discourage Iraq from making further such attacks upon Iranian targets. Iraq was even forced to disperse its warplanes to friendly neighboring nations to keep them from being destroyed.

Iran's gains put it in a position to launch an invasion of its own into Iraqi territory in the summer of 1982. Fearing such an attack was imminent, the UN Security Council passed a resolution in July of that year calling for a cease-fire and a return to

Iran's largest oil refinery at Abadan burns following Iraqi attacks. Iran responded by decimating Iraqi oil refineries with massive air attacks.

the previous borders by both sides. Iraq had indicated a willingness to negotiate an end to the conflict as early as the first few weeks of the war. Hussein had even offered to fully withdraw his troops from Iran and claimed to have done so, although in fact some Iraqi forces remained in Iran. However, Iran refused to cease hostilities unless Saddam Hussein was removed from power. Steeped in fervent Islamic belief, the leaders of Iran believed they were engaged in a jihad, or holy war, and must fight to victory or sacrifice themselves trying. Therefore, Iran rejected the UN's call for a cease-fire.

HUSSEIN UNDER SIEGE

In July 1982 the war entered a new phase when Iran, with five divisions, crossed the border in the south with the objective of capturing the city of Basra, Iraq's second-largest city and its only major port. Basra was considered strategically vital by both sides, and with its predominantly Shia populace, the city looked vulnerable. Iran believed that if it could turn massive numbers of Iraqi Shia in that area against Hussein's government, it would stand a much better chance of capturing the area, in the process shutting off Iraq's access to the Persian Gulf. Iraq, knowing how crippling the loss of Basra would be, counterattacked with four divisions of its own.

The ensuing fighting was of nothing less than historic proportions. As Hiro described it, "some 130,000 troops were locked into the largest infantry fighting since the Second World War."[33] The advantage shifted back and forth. At one point Iran held 120 square miles of Iraqi territory, but by the end of July Iraq had regained most of that. Still, Iranian forces did hold positions close enough to Basra to allow them to maintain heavy, sustained shelling of the city, which it proceeded to do at frequent

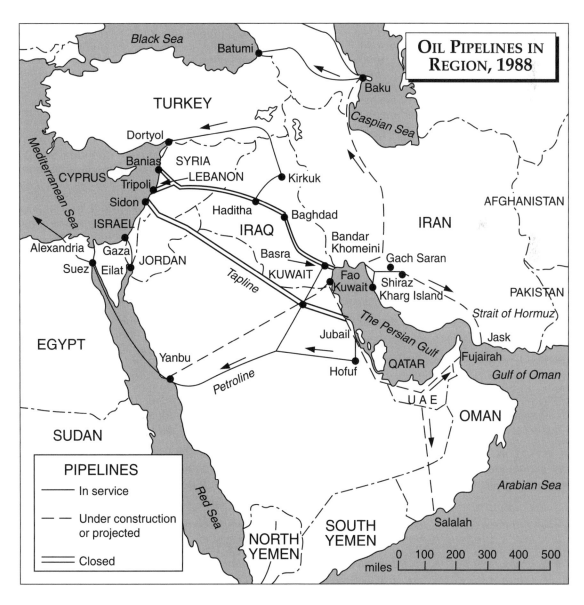

intervals throughout the war. Taking Basra would remain a primary objective of Iran's for the rest of the war.

At the same time, Iran also launched full-scale offensives in the central border area, near the Iraqi capital of Baghdad, again using the tactic of human-wave assaults. Despite the cost in terms of Iranian casualties, however, these efforts resulted in few long-term gains. For example, Iran's forces were able to occupy the Iraqi town of Mandali, sixty-five miles northeast of Baghdad, but they were expelled after a few days. The net effect of this offensive was that Iran won back several square miles of its own territory that Iraq had previously occupied.

However, Iranian forces did not succeed in making deep penetrations into Iraq. Further, the tactics used by Iran virtually ensured that, even when they made territorial gains, they would lose massive numbers of fighters. This was illustrated especially clearly in the fighting that took place in southern Iraq in July: Iran lost over twenty thousand troops killed, injured, or captured, while Iraq lost fewer than ten thousand. However, as Wright points out, "With three times Iraq's population, Tehran could afford higher losses. In fact, according to Khomeini, casualties were not a loss but an asset. Death was honorable, even desirable, when fighting injustice. 'We should sacrifice all our loved ones for the sake of Islam,' Khomeini urged."[34]

In contrast, heavy casualties were a great concern for Hussein. He feared that excessive human losses would turn public opinion against the war, costing him popularity and raising the possibility that he might even be deposed. The purely monetary costs of the war also threatened to erode public support for Hussein. The strong economic growth Iraq had been enjoying prior to the war was impeded by the damage to its oil-producing capability and by the sheer expense of the war effort. With its only Gulf port, Basra, blockaded by Iran's navy and under periodic bombardment, Iraq was highly dependent upon an overland pipeline through Syria to move oil exports. Having aligned itself with Iran in the conflict, Syria cut off the pipeline, compounding Iraq's economic woes.

The combination of Iranian military incursions and economic problems caused declining morale among both Iraq's military and the general population. As a consequence, when the Islamic Conference Organization, a group of predominantly Muslim nations, offered to mediate the conflict in March 1982, Hussein eagerly accepted. But Iran's leaders took this move as a sign of weakness on Hussein's part and became convinced they had gained an advantage in the conflict. That perception was reinforced later that same month, when a new offensive by Iraq in Khuzestan to capture Susangard, a key Iranian town it had failed to take in previous offensives, was rebuffed yet again.

Doubts about Hussein's effectiveness as a leader were spreading both internally and among leaders of other Arab nations who had backed Iraq. Opposition among militant Shiites in Iraq had also grown and become violent. Riots occurred in predominantly Shia areas of the south in May 1982, and in July, Shia militants within Iraq's armed forces even tried to assassi-

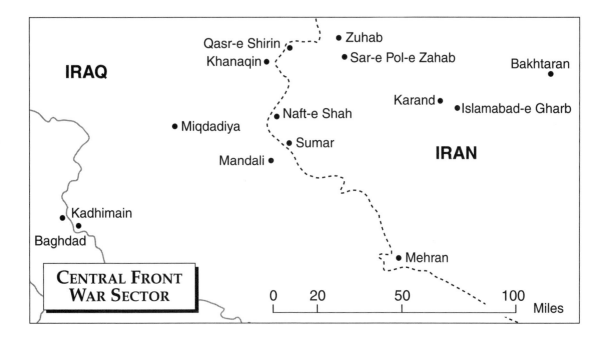

Map labels: Qasr-e Shirin, Khanaqin, Zuhab, Sar-e Pol-e Zahab, Bakhtaran, IRAQ, Karand, Islamabad-e Gharb, Naft-e Shah, Miqdadiya, Sumar, IRAN, Mandali, Kadhimain, Baghdad, Mehran

CENTRAL FRONT WAR SECTOR

0   20   50   100   Miles

nate Hussein, ambushing his motorcade and killing ten of his bodyguards.

Although Hussein survived the attack, his troubles were compounded when Iran launched a new offensive in October and November in the southern and central border regions that cost Iraq heavily in terms of tanks and warplanes. Iran also captured many oil fields on the Iraqi side of the border. Iranian forces were also once again threatening Mandali, the capture of which would have posed a serious threat to Baghdad itself. More than two years after Iraq's first incursions over the border, now it was Iran that seemed to have gained an advantage in the conflict.

IRAQ RECOVERS, RESPONDS

In the long run, Iran's success actually worked to Hussein's advantage. Just as Iraq's invasion had helped Khomeini's government galvanize public support in Iran, Hussein was able to utilize the Iranian threat to build popular support for the war effort among Iraq's citizens.

Helping Hussein was the fact that he was able to continue providing Iraqis with a high level of consumer goods and services by obtaining billions of dollars' worth of credit, mostly from fellow Arab countries in the region. Besides obtaining direct financial assistance, Iraq also made arrangements with its other neighbors to transport oil over their territory, a capability it had lost when Syria shut off its pipeline. These nations did this largely out of fear of Iran. Iranian president Ali Khamenei had displayed clear hostility to the leaders of these nations, calling them "greedy pigs [who] know nothing but satisfying their lust," and threatening to "destroy all the dwarfs if they continue to support falsehood against right."[35] By contrast, Hussein seemed to be a defender of and advocate for Arab interests, since he had publicly stated his sense of responsibility for the defense of all Arab peoples. For example, when war against Iran seemed imminent, he had addressed Iraqi troops, saying, "Our duty extends to every part of the Arab homeland and to everywhere our hand reaches to maintain the Arab honor."[36]

At the same time, Hussein sought to defuse Iranian claims that he was an enemy of Islam. To that end, he undertook a

HUSSEIN AND PAN-ARABISM

Pan-Arabism is a modern movement that has grown out of historic principles of Arab unity and independence from foreign influences. Saddam Hussein and the Iraqi Baaths were among the earliest proponents of Pan-Arabism in the post–World War II era and actively promoted Iraq as a leader among Arabs. There was once talk of several different Arab nations, including Egypt, Syria, Jordan, and Iraq, unifying into a single nation. However, differences developed between the governments that prevented this.

Still, Saddam Hussein drew heavily upon the concept of Arab unity in trying to get international support in the Iran-Iraq War. Hussein often made statements about fighting the war on behalf of all the Arab peoples against their cultural and ethnic rivals. In their book *Iran and Iraq at War*, Shahram Chubin and Charles Tripp quote Hussein during the time leading up to the Iran-Iraq War, when he was massively building up Iraq's military: "Iraq is building an army not to defend just its own borders, but to serve as the shield and sword of the Arab nation against its enemies." However, some Arab leaders feared that Hussein's quest for Arab unity, combined with his large-scale military buildup, indicated that he wanted to gain power in other Arab nations at their expense. To help enlist critical support in his war with Iran, Hussein sought to reassure other Arab nations about his intentions. Two years into the war, he made this statement, quoted in Dilip Hiro's *The Longest War*, which essentially contradicted the basic principal of Pan-Arabism: "The principal of linking unity to the removal of boundaries is no longer acceptable to the present Arab mentality. . . . The Arab reality is that the Arabs are now 22 states, and we have to behave accordingly." The willingness to be so flexible in adapting and changing policies earned Saddam Hussein a reputation as a leader who is highly opportunistic and pragmatic as well as ruthlessly forceful.

public relations campaign in which he openly displayed a devotion to Islam, something he had previously seemed indifferent to. Dilip Hiro gives some details of these efforts: "The example of Saddam Hussein praying in different mosques under the glare of television lights was emulated by other Baathist figures. In March 1982 the Iraqi leader made it a point to offer prayers on [historic Islamic leader] Imam Ali's birthday."[37] Shia clerics and other religious leaders were recruited to express support for Hussein and Iraq's war effort. Hussein also referred to Arabs' traditional ties to Islam as justification for Iraq's actions, pointing out that it was the Arabs who "carried and defended the banner of Islam until it reached the furthest corners of the earth, including [Iran]."[38] Hussein also claimed that it was in fact he who was fighting a jihad—a war on behalf of God and Islam.

The Iraqi leader also worked to blunt opposition from within his own military. He conferred extensively with military commanders and reached accommodation with them by giving assurances that they would have greater control over tactics and strategy. In addition, Hussein worked to improve relations with other nations that could provide weapons and war material. He offered favorable terms for obtaining Iraqi oil to major industrial powers in exchange for hard currency and cooperation in obtaining military supplies. Hussein also made efforts to improve his nation's image among those nations, many of which had regarded Iraq as a rogue state since the overthrow of the monarchy in 1958. With Iran continuing to be estranged from the world's major industrial and military powers and unwilling to heed international calls for an end to the conflict, Iraq had a great advantage in its ability to obtain modern weapons and equipment.

By November 1982 Hussein had succeeded to a point where he was able to vividly demonstrate a high level of national support for his leadership. Hiro describes the events of that month:

> On November 9 [Hussein] bravely proposed referendums in Iran and Iraq to determine who was more popular in his own country: Khomeini or Saddam Hussein. The next day he declared that Iran was trying to overthrow the Baghdad regime not because "a certain person . . . was in the regime" but because it wanted to "control all of Iraq." On November 13 an informal referendum materialized in Baghdad when reportedly some four million people participated in huge demonstrations. Carrying pictures of Saddam Hussein, the marchers shouted, "Yes, yes Saddam/This is the referendum." . . . These events had an uplifting impact on the Iraqi forces at the front.[39]

Iraqi morale was also boosted by improved military fortunes. When Iran sent one hundred thousand troops over the border in the southern region in an attempt to capture the Basra-Baghdad highway near the Iraqi city Amara, Iraqi forces, making effective use of warplanes and helicopters, pushed the invaders back and inflicted heavy losses upon them. Another attempt by Iran to capture

THE KURDS: A PEOPLE WITH NO HOMELAND

Culturally distinctive from both the Arabs who dominate Iraq and from the Iranians, the Kurds represent a significant ethnic minority in both countries. Historically, the Kurds have been a mostly nomadic people, although now the great majority have settled into towns or on farms. The Kurds have developed a different language and many distinctive customs that differentiate them from any of the local nationalities. There are an estimated 25 million Kurds worldwide, but the majority of them live in Iran, Iraq, and eastern Turkey.

There is a province in northwestern Iran called Kurdistan, but there has never been an independent state or entity by that name. Generally, Kurdistan is used to refer to an area that includes eastern Turkey, northern Iraq, and northwestern Iran. After the end of World War I, an agreement called the Treaty of Sevres committed the European powers and the nations of southwestern Asia to allow for the creation of an independent Kurdistan. However, the treaty was never ratified. After World War II, Kurdistan in Iran enjoyed some autonomy for a short time under the protection of the Soviet Union. However, the Western allies and the Iranian government pressured the Soviets to withdraw from Iran. And so today, as for all of history, the Kurds have no homeland.

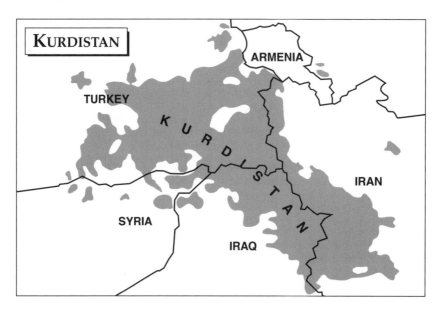

In early 1983 the Iranians twice attempted to capture the Basra-Baghdad highway but both times were repulsed with heavy casualties.

control of the strategic highway in April was also turned back, once again with heavy Iranian casualties.

Still, Iraqi efforts to regain an advantage in the ground war failed. In between the two Iranian offensives that Iraq turned back in early 1983, Iraq launched an unsuccessful offensive of its own in the central sector of the border region. With the war now well into its third year, neither side was close to victory. Combined combat fatalities were at about one hundred thousand, and all indications were that fierce fighting would continue. Stalemate was the most apt description that could be made of the status of the war at this stage. It appeared increasingly likely that only outside intervention would significantly change that status, but with worldwide oil supplies barely affected by the war and no sign that the violence would spread beyond the two combatants, most nations showed little concern or interest in getting involved. That was about to change.

4 Boldness and Backlash: The World Takes Sides

During the early years of the Iran-Iraq War, most of the world saw little to be gained from getting involved in the dispute and even some advantage in a continuation of the conflict. This attitude was reflected in the comments of a Middle East researcher in 1984: "There is little to choose between the belligerents. . . . Humanitarian considerations aside, most third parties may therefore prefer the indefinite prolongation of an inconclusive war since their paramount concern is the mutual neutralization of Iran and Iraq."[40] Regardless of the low regard in which both countries might be held, a series of events that began in the summer of 1983 greatly increased international interest and involvement in the Iran-Iraq War. This led to higher levels of international assistance to the warring countries (mainly Iraq); larger military contingents from major nations, especially the United States, in the Persian Gulf; and intensive efforts by other nations and international organizations to achieve peace.

Among the events that brought greater worldwide attention to the conflict were major battlefield successes by the Iranians, stirring fears that Iran might ultimately emerge triumphant in the war. Given the hostility that Khomeini had already displayed toward them, the major industrialized nations feared that should Iran become the dominant military power in the Persian Gulf, the flow of oil from the region would be disrupted. There were also indications that Iran was starting to target violence at other nations that were assisting Iraq. For example, a multibomb terrorist attack in Kuwait appeared to be the work of Iranian-allied militants. For its part, Iraq disturbed the international community by using chemical weapons against Iranian troops.

THE WORLD BECOMES WARY

Worldwide uneasiness over the war started to grow when, in 1983, with the cooperation of Iraqi Kurds, Iranian troops made deep penetrations into northern Iraq and captured two major strategic locations, the peak of Mount Karman and the garrison town Hajj Umran. In mountainous terrain, the tanks and attacks with planes and helicopters that the Iraqis had used to repel other recent Iranian offensives were largely ineffective, and Iran was better able to hold positions it captured. This success led to further Iranian offensives in this region in coordination with the Kurds. Launched in the fall of 1983, these gained the Iranians additional territory. As a bonus, the presence of Iranian troops severed links between Iraq and Iran's own Kurdish dissidents.

It was in response to Iran's Kurdistan incursion that Iraq first used chemical weapons. Soon thereafter, evidence emerged that Iraq was also using these weapons in battling the Iranians in the south. The use of such weapons was specifically banned under an international agreement known as the 1925 Geneva Protocol, which Iraq had officially agreed to observe. The UN Security Council issued a statement in March 1984 that indicated the degree to which international concern over the Iran-Iraq War, particularly the use of chemical weapons, was growing:

> [The Security Council members] note with particular concern . . . that chemical weapons have been used. Furthermore, they express their grave concern about all reported violations in the conflict of the rules of international law and of the principles and rules of international conduct accepted by the world community to prevent or alleviate the human suffering of warfare.[41]

Still, despite its members' condemnation of Iraqi actions, the Security Council took no meaningful action to punish Iraq or prevent future use of chemical weapons.

A Kurdish women recovers in a hospital from the effects of an Iraqi chemical weapons attack.

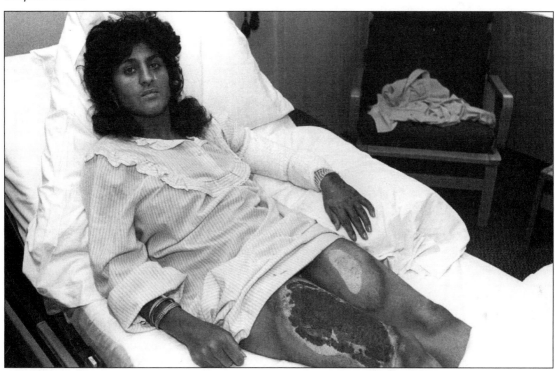

Justifying Jihad

During the Iran-Iraq War, both sides claimed they were engaging in a jihad or holy war in the name of Islam. The term jihad has come to denote violence in recent times, but it has more traditionally referred to general struggle and striving on behalf of Allah, or God. Those who commit acts of horrid violence distort the spirit and meaning of jihad, but the Koran, Islam's holy book, does speak about war, providing several situations where it is acceptable and even desirable. This passage from sura (chapter) 2 of the Koran is especially relevant to the issue of justification of war:

"Fight in the Cause of Allah,
Those who fight you,
But do not transgress limits;
For Allah loveth not transgressors

And slay them
Wherever ye catch them,
And turn them out
From where they have
Turned you out;
For tumult and oppression
Are worse than slaughter . . .

But if these cease
Allah is oft forgiving,
Most merciful.

And fight them on
Until there is no more
Tumult or oppression,
And there prevail
Justice and faith in Allah;
But if they cease,
Let there be no hostility
Except to those
Who practice oppression."

International reaction to Iraq's use of chemical weapons might have been stronger if the prospect of an Iranian victory had not seemed so ominous. Moreover, Iran was immediately suspected of being behind the five-bomb explosions in Kuwait in December 1983. These bombings had seemed clearly aimed at Western interests, since their targets included the U.S. and French embassies, and those who carried out the attacks were suspected of being associated with the Khomeini-allied organization Al Daawa.

In addition to its continuing open hostility toward Western powers, Iran's government also maintained its antagonism toward the Arab nations of the Persian Gulf region. Although Iranian president Khamenei tempered his rhetoric, saying Iran had no wish to fight the Persian Gulf States as long as they stayed out of the conflict, his nation's attitude could hardly be described as friendly. As the journal *Foreign Affairs* noted, "In a systematic hate campaign, the Iranian media continuously denounced [Kuwait and Saudi Arabia] and charged them with allowing Iraq to use their bases to attack Iran. Violence-prone antigovernment groups in the two countries were . . . consistently praised in the Iranian media."[42]

Another action taken by Iran that riled the Western powers, especially the United States, was a threat it made late in 1983 to close the Strait of Hormuz, the narrow passage that offers the only entry for ships into the Persian Gulf. Iran made this threat in response to repeated and intensifying air attacks by Iraq against Iran's Kharg Island oil refinery, located in the Persian Gulf. Iraq had first targeted Kharg Island in 1982, but attacked the facility more frequently and heavily after receiving increased weapons shipments from foreign suppliers. Iran's revolutionary parliamentary speaker, Ali Akbar Hashemi Rafsanjani, made a connection between the Iraqi attacks and the supplies Iraq was receiving from foreign nations in justifying Iran's threat to close the Strait of Hormuz: "If Iran's oil shipping were halted, then no country in the world would be able to use Persian Gulf oil."[43] The threat to close this passageway went directly against a publicly stated U.S. policy of keeping the strait open to international shipping at any cost.

THE MAJNOON OFFENSIVE

Not long after, just how dangerous a foe Iran had become was manifested when, in February 1984, it undertook what was known as the Majnoon offensive, named after Iraqi islands located in a thick marshy area in southern Iraq called Haur al Hawizeh. The Majnoon Islands contained thousands of oil wells and presented Iran with a tempting target. Yet Iraq considered this area safe: Attacking forces would have to cross the Tigris River and deal with marshy terrain and thick vegetation. Believing the Haur al Hawizeh impenetrable, Iraq had not deployed forces to defend it. But the Iranians used unconventional means, such as helicopters, rubber rafts, and small motorboats to move troops into the area. They also used infantry on foot and mounted on motorcycles to cover narrow strips of land through the marshes. Like the mountainous terrain in the northern Kurdish area, the soggy conditions in Haur al Hawizeh rendered the heavy armor that had been so helpful to Iraq's military in other regions nearly useless.

The lack of defensive capability and the strong element of surprise allowed Iran to capture the Majnoon Islands after just two days of fighting. Wright describes this Iranian incursion into Iraq as "important because the Tigris crossing demonstrated how deeply Iran was capable of penetrating inside Iraq and because [Majnoon] is among the richest of Iraq's oil fields."[44] Furthermore, capturing the Majnoon Islands put the Iranians in a good position to capture the town of Al Qurnah, which was strategically located

The bodies of Iraqi soldiers whom the Iranians blindfolded, tied up, and executed lie in a mass grave following the Majnoon offensive.

at the head of the Shatt al Arab. Capturing Al Qurnah would also give Iran control of a pivotal point along the highway linking Baghdad to Basra, essentially enabling Iran to cut Iraq in two.

After recovering from their initial shock, the Iraqis were able to mount a defense that prevented Iranian forces from taking Al Qurnah, but they were unable to expel them from most of the territory they had taken in the marshes. Just how vital this territory was for both sides was demonstrated by the fact that at its peak the fighting involved as many as half a million troops and cost over twenty-five thousand lives. Once again, Iraq used chemical weapons in this battle. As in the past, this tactic caused great displeasure among other nations, but international uneasiness over the prospect of an Iranian victory tended to mute protest against Iraq's actions.

A WIDELY DIVERGENT COALITION

As Iraq came under increasing military pressure, Hussein's international diplomatic and public relations efforts came to play an increasingly significant part in the war. The nations that had provided Iraq with the most support were other Arab nations who felt threatened by Iran's advocacy of militant Islamic government. Many of the Arab nations in the Persian Gulf region had significant numbers of Shia inhabitants, and by and large these Shia were economically and socially disadvantaged compared to their Sunni counterparts. The Sunni rulers in these nations feared that the Shia segments of their populations could be especially receptive and responsive to Iran's calls for Islamic revolutionary action. However, these nations were not natural allies of Iraq's either. Since the Iraqi revolution in 1958, many of these countries had had strained relations with Iraq, stemming from Iraq's promotion of socialism and its support for the unification of all Arab peoples into a single state. And since the 1958 Iraqi revolution had overthrown a monarchy, nations in the region such as Saudi Arabia and Kuwait, which were still ruled by monarchs, were bound to be wary of Iraq.

CHEMICAL WEAPONS

The use of chemical weapons by Iraq in its war with Iran was a grave concern among nations throughout the world. The destruction these weapons could cause was made apparent by their use in World War I, when their use resulted in horrific burns, sores, lesions, infections, debilitating diseases, and even death among those exposed to them. In order to prevent chemical weapons usage in future wars, representatives from a multitude of nations met in Geneva, Switzerland, to commit their countries to a prohibition against the use of chemical weapons in warfare. Iraq and Iran were both among the nations that officially agreed to the prohibition.

The international agreement banning the use of chemical weapons is known as the Geneva Protocol. It was signed in 1925 and became effective in 1928. It prohibited the use of a wide variety of chemical weapons, including toxic gases, asphyxiants, liquid poisons, and bacteriological weapons.

Hussein therefore worked hard to stress the themes of Arab unity and common interest that he had espoused since before the start of the war. His efforts are described by authors Shahram Chubin and Charles Tripp in *Iran and Iraq at War:*

> Saddam Hussein has . . . devoted considerable energy to . . . persuading his regional neighbors that they share a community of interest with Iraq in its attempts to thwart . . . the Iranian armed forces and to bring the war to an end. On one level, this has meant the identification of Iraq's cause with the larger pan-Arab cause, thus creating obligations for those who claim to subscribe to [pan-Arabism]. On another level, it has taken the form of a direct appeal to the self-interest of certain Arab rulers, threatening them with the probable consequences of an Iraqi military collapse, and simultaneously promising them the financial or political gifts which Iraq still has at its disposal.[45]

Hussein succeeded in making nations like Saudi Arabia and Kuwait, which had supported and assisted Iraq mostly as a means of containing Iran, feel more comfortable with his regime and increase their assistance. Saudi Arabia came forward with offers of economic aid to foreign companies supplying Iraq with goods and services, and also made up shortfalls in oil supplies that the war had caused for Iraqi customers. Both Saudi Arabia and Kuwait loaned Iraq billions of dollars. Kuwait also sent large truck caravans into Iraq on a daily basis, loaded with both civilian and military goods and supplies.

Other Arab countries offered Iraq new support. After it signed a peace treaty with Israel in 1978, Egypt had been harshly criticized and ostracized by Iraq and the rest of the Arab world. But the severe threat posed by Iran and Hussein's eagerness to forge new international alliances made reconciliation possible, and Iraq bought about $2.7 dollars' worth of arms and ammunition from Egypt during the first half of the war. In addition, Egypt sent military instructors to Iraq and allowed Hussein's government to conscript Egyptians living in Iraq into the Iraqi army.

Support for Iraq from Arab nations also came in the form of diplomatic efforts and maneuvering. In March 1984 a group of Persian Gulf nations known as the Gulf Cooperation Council (GCC) called upon members of the Arab League, an international organization of Arab states, to stop selling arms and military supplies to Iran. This action represented a shift in the GCC's attitude. The council had originally offered to mediate the conflict, but after Iran rejected that offer, the GCC's position tilted decidedly in favor of Iraq.

SUPPORT FROM WESTERN EUROPE

Support from its fellow Arab states surely helped Iraq, but of greater significance was the growing support coming from major Western powers. Initially these nations had professed neutrality in the war, but as early as 1982 France had taken a definitive stance supporting Iraq. In November of that year, French president François Mitterand declared, "We do not wish Iraq to be defeated in this war."[46] Pointing out the extreme dan-

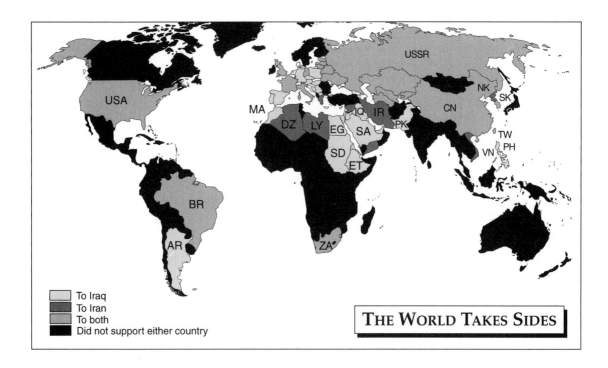

To Iraq
To Iran
To both
Did not support either country

THE WORLD TAKES SIDES

ger that an Iranian victory would present to the West's allies in the Persian Gulf region, France urged other Western nations to join it in providing support to Iraq.

For the previous twenty years, most of Iraq's military supplies had come from the Soviet Union. But in the early 1980s, France became an equally important provider of weapons to Iraq. Some of France's support for Iraq is described in *Iraq: From Sumer to Saddam:*

> In 1981 French Arms sales to Iraq were $2.148 billion; in 1982 $1.925 billion; and in 1983 $2 billion. Helicopters and Mirage F-1 fighter-bombers were being supplied, and France also agreed to lend Iraq five Super Etendard aircraft equipped to carry Exocet air-to-surface missiles. . . . [An estimate] suggests that France sold Iraq arms to the value of $56

billion during the period of the 1980s Gulf War.[47]

The Super Etendard planes and Exocet missiles were among the most advanced weapons of the time, strongly demonstrating France's military commitment to Iraq.

Economic relations between France and Iraq were similarly strong. Over one thousand French companies were doing business in Iraq by 1983, and thousands of French civilian and military experts in various fields were based there. As the war strained Iraq's finances, the French government offered Iraq relief in the form of rescheduled loans and accepted partial payments in the form of oil, which Saudi Arabia supplied. While providing extensive assistance to Iraq, France also became a vocal advocate of prohibiting the sale of arms and munitions to the Iranian regime.

THE CARTER DOCTRINE

The U.S. naval action in the Persian Gulf during the Iran-Iraq War was founded on a policy called the Carter Doctrine. It asserted that the United States would take any action necessary, including military, to assure safe international passage in the Persian Gulf. In his 1980 State of the Union speech, which was reproduced in the January 24 issue of the *New York Times* that year, Carter proclaimed this policy, specifically citing "outside forces" as the threat to be protected against. However, Carter also spoke of Western dependence on the region's oil supplies and the political instability that had erupted in Iran in discussing the U.S. willingness to use force to keep the Persian Gulf open. After becoming president in 1981, Reagan reaffirmed the Carter Doctrine as U.S. policy. Reagan also built upon the doctrine by explicitly including U.S. military action as an option to be used in any situation that might disrupt free access to shipping in the Gulf. Carter cited the following threats as justification for projecting U.S. power in the Persian Gulf region:

- the steady growth and increased projection of Soviet military power beyond its own borders;

- the overwhelming dependence of the Western democracies on oil supplies from the Middle East;

- the press of social, religious, economic, and political change in the many nations of the developing world, exemplified by the revolution in Iran.

Against these circumstances, Carter made an assertion of U.S. intentions: Any attempt by any outside force to gain control of the Persian Gulf region will be regarded as an assault on the vital interests of the United States of America. And such an assault will be repelled by any means necessary, including military force.

UNUSUAL ALLIANCE OF SUPERPOWERS

Interestingly, both the United States and the Soviet Union, the two major world superpowers who usually found themselves on opposing sides in regional conflicts, found it worth their while to support Iraq, although for different reasons. Initially, the Soviets had been receptive to the new revolutionary government in Iran. But relations had quickly taken a negative turn. The Soviet Union's invasion of Afghanistan, a Muslim nation, at the end of 1979 was largely responsible for this, as Iran condemned the Soviets' militarism and supported Afghani resistance fighters. Also, the Soviets took a dim view of the Iranian government's suppression of the Iranian Communist Party as part of a general crackdown on dissent. Furthermore, once it became clear that Iran intended to spread its brand of Islamic fundamentalism and revolution, the Soviet Union worried how this might impact upon its republics in Central Asia, such as Turkmenistan and Kazakhstan, that were home to large Muslim populations. Finally, the Soviet Union denounced Iran's persistent refusals to settle the war peacefully, claiming they provided the United States and its allies with an excuse to intervene in the area militarily and prevented Arab and other Muslim nations from forming a united front against Israel. In 1983 the Soviet Union reached new agreements with Iraq that provided $2 billion worth of new warplanes, missiles, and tanks to the Iraqis. A large number of Soviet military advisers were also sent to Iraq under these agreements.

For its part, the United States had an overriding interest in keeping the Strait of Hormuz open in order to maintain adequate oil supplies for itself and its allies. U.S. president Ronald Reagan demonstrated his willingness to use force for this purpose by deploying thirty U.S. warships to the area. The United States was also adamantly opposed to the spread of Islamic fundamentalism in the Persian Gulf region. The evidence that Iran was assisting Islamic terrorists gave the United States further incentive to act against Iran, especially when 259 American marines stationed in Lebanon were killed in a bombing of their barracks—an attack for which the U.S. government blamed Iran.

Although the United States remained officially neutral, U.S. defense secretary Caspar Weinberger openly indicated a concern over the prospect of an Iranian victory. "We want to see the war end in a way that doesn't destabilize the area," Weinberger said, adding, "an Iranian victory is certainly not in our interests."[48] Accordingly, the United States took a number of measures to bolster Iraq. The United States provided satellite, radar, and other intelligence to Saudi Arabia, which that nation passed on to the Iraqi government. Diplomatic contacts between the United States and Iraq, which had been strained by American support for Israel, were stepped up, and the two nations resumed full diplomatic ties late in 1984. When full diplomatic relations between the United States and Iraq were established, intelligence that had been previously routed through the Saudis was provided directly to Iraq. The United States also provided

Iraq with nonmilitary supplies, including helicopters that were supposedly intended for civilian use but that could be converted to military applications.

More important than providing direct aid, in November 1982 the United States re- moved Iraq from a list of nations that it claimed supported international terrorism and placed Iran on that same list in January 1984. This effectively made arms sales to Iraq more feasible, while outlawing such sales to Iran by U.S. companies. At the same

ARMS SHIPMENTS TO IRAQ

Nation	U.S. Dollar Amount	Arms
Argentina	$40 million (1985)	Pucara jet trainers
Brazil	$300 million (1979–84)	Tucano turboprop trainers, antiair missiles, missile launchers, mobile rocket launchers, armored fighting vehicles, jeeps
Czechoslovakia	$400 million (1980–86)	
Chile	$120 million (1985–87)	cluster bombs
Egypt	$1–3 billion (1980–86)	Saggers, T-55s, F-6s, F-7s
France	$56 billion (1980–86)	Mirage F-1s, Super-Etendards, Super-Frelon helicopters, SA-342 Gazelle and SA-316B helicopters, Roland-2s, Exocet missiles, AMX-30 tanks (Note: Around 15% of France's total arms production was intended for Iraq.)
Federal Republic of Germany	$140 million (1979–83)	BO-105 helicopters, electrical and navigational equipment, military radio
Greece	$15 million (?) (1984–86)	Contract for repair and overhaul of jet aircraft, grenades, light arms
Italy	$410 million (+ $1.8 billion for 7 corvettes) (1979–83)	helicopters, 155 mm ammunition, floating dock
People's Republic of China	$1.5 billion (1979–83)	T-69 tanks
Poland	$850 million (1979–83)	T-55 tanks
Rumania	$400 million (1979–83)	Contract for repair and maintenance of armored vehicles and weapons, helicopters
Switzerland	$5 million (?) (1984)	PC-7 turbo trainers
United Kingdom	$280 million (1979–80)	Chieftain tanks, armored fighting vehicles, military trucks, pilot training
U.S.S.R.	$10 billion	MiGs (21, 23, 25, 29), SU-20s, Tu-22s, T-55, 62, 72 tanks, armored fighting vehicles, artillery, SA-6, 8, 0 SAMs, military advisers and trainers

time the United States also undertook a diplomatic effort, called Operation Staunch, to discourage other Western nations from sending arms to Iran.

BENEFITS OF INTERNATIONAL SUPPORT

The many forms of international support Iraq received were of enormous importance in countering the advantages Iran possessed in terms of population, strategic location, and size. By 1983 Iraq was outperforming Iran in the air, allowing the Iraqis to blunt at least some of Iran's ground offensives. Even though Iran made substantial advances during the Majnoon offensive, analysts believe that Iraq's air superiority prevented Iran from taking even more territory. In other cases, the intelligence provided by Saudi Arabia and the United States helped Iraq gain advance knowledge of Iranian attacks and deploy its troops effectively to defend against them.

The planes and missiles acquired by Iraq were also used in the frequent attacks launched against the Kharg Island oil facility. Kharg was protected by some of Iran's strongest air defenses, which at first kept damage to the facility by Iraq's attacks to a minimum. But when the Iraqis began using their newly acquired French Super Etendard planes and Exocet missiles in the attacks in 1984, Kharg sustained more serious damage.

The heightened attacks against Kharg Island were one of several new developments that represented an intensification of the conflict. Up until the beginning of 1984, the important action in the conflict had largely been confined to direct combat on the ground and relatively close to the Iran-Iraq border. Attacks against targets in the Persian Gulf or directly affecting other nations had been limited and in any case had not had a strong bearing on the course of the war. But with neither side able to make a decisive breakthrough on the ground after three and a half years, both Iran and Iraq began seeking other means of gaining an advantage.

PERSISTENT PEACE EFFORTS

As the war intensified, so too did efforts by third parties to settle the dispute. Such efforts were not unprecedented, of course. In addition to peace proposals put forth by the UN and the GCC, there had also been numerous and frequent other attempts to achieve a cease-fire between Iran and Iraq, coming almost entirely from small or nonaligned nations or international organizations made up of such nations. Charles Hume, a diplomat who was involved with UN efforts to end the war, describes some of these early peacemaking attempts:

> Iraq . . . agreed on October 5 [1980] to the proposal by Pakistan's president Zia ul-Haq . . . for a unilateral three day cease-fire. . . . On October 16 Iraq accepted a proposal by Habib Chatti, secretary-general of the Islamic Conference, for negotiations. In addition, there were the PLO [Palestine Liberation Organization] (both sides had rejected its October 4 four-point plan) and a nonaligned peace

A cargo ship prepares to dock at Iran's Kharg Island. The oil facility was the target of Iraqi air raids that did extensive damage in 1984.

mission led by Cuban foreign minister Isidóro Malmierca and including Yugoslavia, India, Zambia, Pakistan, and the PLO.[49]

International desire to end the war increased as the violence escalated and spread, and the more powerful nations of the world became increasingly involved in

the conflict. The top-ranking UN official, secretary general Javier Pérez de Cuéllar, stepped up his mediation efforts. But these efforts were invariably thwarted by Iran's refusal to accept any proposal that failed to include the removal of Hussein from power and the paying of war damages to Iran. Iranian responses to initiatives were typified by President Khamenei's comment after a visit to Tehran in October 1982 by representatives of the Islamic Conference Organization, who were trying to broker a peace deal. He said Iranian forces would "proceed toward Baghdad whenever they deem it necessary."[50]

Hence the war continued. In the ensuing months and years there would be more terrorist attacks, more use of chemical weapons, and more massive battlefield slaughter. As the Iran-Iraq War reached new levels of violence and destruction, other nations were either forced into the fray or found their interests were too much at risk for them to continue to distance themselves from it.

5 War Frontiers Expand

Iraq's intensified attacks against Kharg Island had represented the largest escalation of hostilities yet. To take a further toll on Iran, Iraq expanded its range of targets, attacking civilian population centers as well as production facilities of various kinds on the Iranian mainland. Even more alarming to the rest of the world were Iraq's attacks against oil tankers from other nations as they called at Iranian ports. Iran responded to these attacks with stepped-up activity of its own, targeting the vessels of Iraq's regional Gulf allies, particularly Saudi Arabia and Kuwait. With tensions and violence spreading and intensifying and now spilling over to affect the rest of the world, the Iran-Iraq War became the focus of much more international attention and attempts at intervention.

TURBULENT GULF WATERS

The Iraqi attack on a Panamanian tanker on April 18, 1984, marked the first time Iraq had struck another nation's ship, but over the next several weeks Iraq also struck a Turkish tanker as well as a Saudi ship bound for France and carrying Iranian oil. According to Hiro, the Iraqis were, "sig-nalling their resolve to target all ships, irrespective of their ownership, serving Iranian ports."[51] In late June, Iraq staged repeated attacks on Kharg and on Iranian ships nearby. Iran responded by attacking Kuwaiti oil tankers and a Liberian ship carrying Saudi Arabian oil. Once again, Iranian parliamentary leader Rafsanjani pointed to the support other nations were providing to Iraq in defending Iran's actions, claiming, "If the Persian Gulf were to become unsafe for us, the natural reaction would be to stop Iraq's indirect use by making it unsafe for others."[52]

The uneasiness that took hold among other nations in the region during that time was dramatically demonstrated when Saudi Arabia shot down an Iranian jet fighter over the Gulf, claiming it had violated Saudi air space. The Iranians claimed the plane had been over international waters, and for a time observers feared that Saudi Arabia would become directly involved in the conflict. However, both Iran and Saudi Arabia soon publicly stated they did not wish to engage each other in hostilities.

The failure of the Saudis to join the war was most likely a disappointment for Saddam Hussein. Experts believe his purpose in targeting international shipping—what came to be called the Tanker War—had been to involve other nations in the war to such an extent that Iran would be forced to cease fighting. Hiro explains:

> The overall Iraqi purpose in initiating and sustaining the Tanker War was to make oil shipments from the Gulf hazardous, thus internationalizing the conflict and drawing in the superpowers—and/or getting Saudi Arabia and Kuwait to join the hostilities formally on Baghdad's side. The latter development would have opened up a new front against Iran, severely straining its already depleted air force and torpedoing Iranian plans to mount land offensives against Iraq.[53]

The Tanker War certainly made shipping in the Persian Gulf more hazardous than it had been earlier, but it did not

Clouds of black smoke engulf a burning tanker, which was hit by an Iranian rocket.

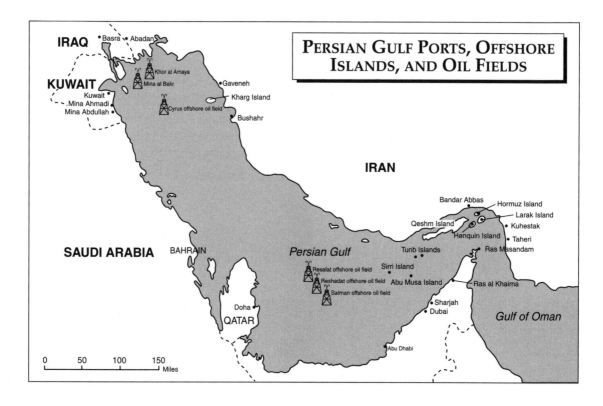

PERSIAN GULF PORTS, OFFSHORE ISLANDS, AND OIL FIELDS

bring as great a response from Saudi Arabia or Kuwait as Iraq had hoped for. The GCC did resolve to offer oil tankers trading with member nations air cover during their passage through the Gulf, and Saudi Arabia set up an air defense zone in the Gulf beyond its own territorial limits. Using radar planes provided by the United States to look for hostile aircraft, Saudi Arabia watched over tankers as they plied the waters of the Persian Gulf. Perhaps the most important result of the outbreak of the Tanker War, however, was that eight U.S. warships began escorting Saudi and Kuwaiti tankers through the Gulf. While the U.S. action was not on the level Saddam Hussein had hoped for, this was only the beginning of a gradual escalation of U.S. involvement in the war.

IRAQI AIR POWER ON THE RISE

Throughout the rest of 1984 and into 1985, Iraq sporadically struck Iranian vessels and Kharg Island. Iraqi activity intensified periodically, as in late 1984, when Iraq claimed to have hit thirty vessels in three months. Meanwhile, the actions taken by various nations to protect ships belonging to Iraq's allies prevented Iran from matching Iraqi aggression in the Gulf waters. By the end of 1985, Iran had managed to strike just over thirty ships in the Gulf, while Iraq's total was well over one hundred.

Iran's Kharg Island oil facility did recover from the damage inflicted by Iraq in early 1984, and Iran refurbished and improved the island's defenses. However, during that time Iraq continued to build up its air force, gaining more planes and equipment with more modern and sophisticated systems. Iraqi air force personnel also became more skilled. This enabled Iraq to mount its most effective attacks yet against Kharg Island in September 1985. The damage inflicted in these attacks cut the facility's production capacity by about a third. Although Iran compensated by adjusting the island's defenses and by ferrying oil from Kharg to other facilities out of range of Iraqi warplanes, ongoing attacks continued to hamper operations at Kharg. Iraq also hit many of the ships transporting oil from Kharg to Iran's more remote Gulf facilities. The escalation of attacks against Iranian targets in Persian Gulf waters were indicative of a new Iraqi strategy, as noted by the *Financial Times* in September 1985:

> Senior Iraqi officials have recently said privately that Baghdad's aim is now to wipe out the Kharg Island facilities completely in a bid to bring an end to the Gulf War. . . . Until August the [Iraqi] strategy was to harass and disrupt oil traffic but not to stop it altogether because of the apprehensions of other Arab oil producers about an escalation of the war.[54]

Iraq aggressively pursued its new strategy in the Gulf beyond Kharg. Iraq's increasing effectiveness in the air was dramatically demonstrated when its planes raided oil facilities that Iran had believed were safely out of range. These raids included an attack on August 12 against Sirri Island, nearly five hundred miles from Iraq's southernmost air base, and another on November 25 against Larak Island in

---

AIR FORCE COMPARISONS

Iraqi Air Force

Personnel: 40,000 (including 10,000 air defense)

Bombers	Tu-22	7–12
	Tu-16	8–10
FGA (11-13 squadrons)		
	MiG-23/27 BM	40–60
	Mirage F-1EQ5 (Exocet-equipped)	20
	Mirage F-1EQ200	23
	Su-7/Su-20	75–90
Interceptors (5 squadrons)		
	MiG-29	1–37(a)
	MiG-25	25
	MiG-19	400
	Mig-21	150–200
	Mirage F-1EQ	30
Reconnaissance (1 squadron)		
	MiG-25	5
Transport (2 squadrons)		
	Various types including Mi-24, SA-342, SA-321, MBB BO-105	150 (?)
Attack Helicopters		
	Various types including An-12, An 26, Il-76	57

Iranian Air Force

Personnel: 35,000

FGA (8 squadrons)		
	F-4D/E	35–20 (?)
	F-5E/F	45–30 (?)
Interceptor (1 squadron)		
	F-14A	14–10 (?)
Reconnaisance (1 squadron)		
	F-14A	5 (?)
	RF-4E	3
Transport (5 squadrons)		
	Various types including C-130E/H, Fokker F-27	41
Attack Helicopters		
	Various types including HH-34F, AB-206A	75–45 (?)

Note: Figures are approximate due to fluctuating availability of operational units.

the Strait of Hormuz, which required a round-trip of nearly twelve hundred miles. How Iraq was able to accomplish this mystified experts at the time and would continue to do so. These missions would have required the planes either to refuel on another nation's soil or refuel in midair, a capability the Iraqis were not known to possess. At the time, Iran accused Saudi Arabia of allowing Iraq to land and refuel on its territory; other observers think Iraq secretly received assistance from the United States or other Western nations to refuel in flight.

Whatever means it used to carry out these long-distance raids, Iraq's air campaign took a toll on Iran economically. By the fall of 1986, Iran's oil exports had fallen to eight hundred thousand barrels per day from a level of about 3.2 million a day before the war with Iraq. In addition to its assaults on Iranian vessels and critical oil facilities in the Gulf, Iraq was also wreaking havoc from the air on much of the Iranian mainland, diminishing Iran's oil-producing capacity even further and inflicting other damage on the nation's industrial facilities. According to Chubin and Tripp, Iraq adapted another new strategy at this time:

> The Iraqi air force concentrated for the first time in a systematic way not simply on Iran's oil-exporting facilities, but also on other economic targets. During 1986 it attacked industrial plants, power generation facilities, communications centers, and hydro-electric schemes with a growing degree of accuracy.[55]

CIVILIAN AND INDUSTRIAL TARGETS

As its air force grew stronger, Iraq greatly escalated its attacks against Iranian cities and other civilian targets. Flush with the success his forces were enjoying, the head of the Iraqi air force went so far as to say that 1986 would be the year when "no hostile target will be safe."[56]

In fact, both sides had been bombarding civilian targets for years. Although Iran had for a time been able to discourage Iraq from launching missiles, Iraq resumed these attacks in late 1982, when it launched Scud missiles at the Iranian town of Dezful and killed twenty-one people. Iraq had also staged air raids numbering in the hundreds in Khuzestan in December 1982 and January 1983. Later in 1983, Iraq had made use of longer-range Scud missiles, newly acquired from the Soviets, to attack Iranian cities and towns.

Iran had responded to these attacks with artillery barrages on Iraqi towns and cities near the border, especially Basra. Although unable to match Iraq in the number of its air raids, Iran had also increased its bombing of Iraqi targets. Various third parties, especially the UN, had tried to convince both sides to halt attacks on civilian areas, yet air strikes by both sides escalated to the point that there were an average of nine hundred combined civilian casualties per week by June 1984.

Faced with this kind of carnage, UN secretary general Pérez de Cuéllar intensified efforts to bring an end to the war. The two sides agreed to halt attacks on urban centers, and UN observers were placed in both nations' capitals to act as monitors of

STATE-SPONSORED TERRORISM

Both Iran and Iraq have at various times been on a list of nations the United States says provide aid to terrorist organizations. Iraq was designated such a state for its support of Palestinian organizations that targeted terrorism against Israel. When Saddam Hussein sought greater Western support for and cooperation with his country, he distanced himself from terrorism and took visible steps to win the favor of the U.S. government. This led to Iraq's removal from the terrorist list in November 1982, and that allowed for the United States to legally provide much greater support for Iraq, especially military support. Iraq was placed back on the list of nations suspected of supporting terrorism in 1990. Among the terrorist attacks believed to be connected to Iraq is the truck bombing at the World Trade Center in February 1993 and an assassination attempt against former president George Bush when he visited Kuwait that same year.

There were indications Iran was connected to terrorism aimed at Western interests in Lebanon and Kuwait in the early 1980s. Iran was also suspected of contributing to an attempted coup in Bahrain and an assassination attempt against the emir of Kuwait. These were among the events that led to the U.S. State Department putting Iran on the list of suspected terrorist nations in January 1984. Since then Iran has also been connected with the taking of hostages from Western nations in Lebanon, and some people have claimed Iran has supported terrorists participating in airline skyjackings and bombings.

the agreement. The agreement was largely adhered to until March 1985, when Iraq staged air raids against a steel plant and an unfinished nuclear power plant. Iran responded by resuming heavy shelling of Basra from its positions in Haur al Hawizeh. A flurry of air raids and missile attacks by both sides ensued, including strikes on Baghdad and Tehran. This stage of the war came to be called the War of the Cities.

Again the UN Secretary General attempted to stop such assaults on civilian populations, and once again, on April 6, both sides agreed to stop these attacks. However, after a suicide bomber tried to assassinate the Kuwaiti monarch on May 25, Iraq blamed Iran and responded with resumed airborne attacks on Iranian cities. Iraq also escalated attacks on ships and facilities in the Persian Gulf, and Iran responded with missile attacks against Baghdad and with new air strikes against ships calling at Saudi and Kuwaiti ports. Both sides also continued targeting oil-production facilities, each trying to weaken the other's ability to utilize its most valuable resource.

Meanwhile, although 1984 saw Iraq gaining a clear advantage in air power, Hussein's army was unable to improve its performance in the ground war. For its part, Iran was also unable to make a breakthrough on the ground. Unusually rainy weather hampered both sides in their offensive ground operations, and as a result fighting turned out to be less intense during 1984 than it had been in earlier years.

Amid this relative lull in ground combat, Iran surprised the rest of the world by considering a peace proposal from Egypt. This marked the first time Iran had not immediately rejected a call for peace. Iran's motivation, seemingly, was growing support among the Iranian public for resolving the conflict with Iraq. Regional religious councils who had direct contact with Khomeini conveyed to him the fact that many Iranians were growing tired of the war and did not consider the campaign against Iraq to be worth the cost. Among those advocating a cease-fire and a withdrawal of Iranian forces from Iraqi territory

INTERNAL IRANIAN OPPOSITION— THE FREEDOM MOVEMENT

Mehdi Bazargan was the first prime minister of Iran after the Islamic Revolution. However, after the seizure of the American embassy and the Iranian government's refusal to act against the hostage takers, Bazargan resigned. He remained the leader of the Islamic Liberation, or Freedom, Movement, a political organization in Iran that had been instrumental in the overthrow of the Shah, but then became increasingly opposed to the Khomeini regime.

During the ruthless and deadly crackdowns on political opposition in the early years after the revolution, Bazargan maintained a high profile and was boldly vocal in his criticism of the government. This put him at great risk. Other former revolutionary government officials who had turned into Khomeini opponents had either been executed or forced to flee the country. Nevertheless, Bazargan made this statement, quoted in Robin Wright's *In the Name of God: The Khomeini Decade*, during an especially harsh period of repression by the government: "What has the ruling elite done besides bring death and destruction, pack the prisons and cemeteries in every city, create long [lines], shortages, high prices, unemployment, poverty, homeless people, repetitious slogans and a dark future?"

Khomeini appointed Mehdi Bazargan (right) as Iran's prime minister following the Islamic Revolution. Bazargan later split with Khomeini, and by 1985 as a member of Iran's Freedom Movement was vocal in his opposition to continuing the war with Iraq.

was the Freedom Movement, the only remaining major political opposition to Khomeini within Iran. Mehdi Bazargan, who had briefly served as Iran's prime minister following the Islamic Revolution and who was now the leader of the Freedom Movement, was daringly vocal in his opposition to the war. He made this statement in June 1985:

As long as the Iraqi soldiers were on our homeland soil, it was an Islamic duty for our fighters to repel them.

But in the summer of 1982 our soldiers entered Iraq, which is against the principles of Islam. I explained this last year to Imam Khomeini. . . . I also told him that for political and military reasons we should already have negotiated when we were in a position of force, just after our successful counteroffensives in the spring of 1982.[57]

Such open dissent was risky. Others who had opposed the government, even those who, like Bazargan, had once been associated with Khomeini, had been either exiled or executed. The possibility that Bazargan could suffer a similar fate loomed when a pro-government Iranian paper responded to his statement by saying, "Be careful, Mr. Bazargan, your attitude is exhausting the Iranian Islamic people's patience."[58] Bazargan survived, but in spite of signs of growing internal opposition to the war and urging from some of his advisers to reconsider Iran's stance, Khomeini himself continued to support the war. And so the fighting continued.

Iran continued to pursue ground offensives, with Iraq sporadically mounting counterattacks or initiating offensives of its own. From early 1984 through 1985, Iran launched numerous limited offensives in the northern and central areas. In the summer of 1984 and again in the fall of 1985, working in conjunction with Iraqi Kurds, Iran captured additional territory in the north. In the summer and fall of 1984, small-scale offensives in the central border area helped Iran recapture several dozen square miles of territory it had previously lost to Iraq. But the heaviest fighting took place in the southern area, in and around the Haur al Hawizeh marshes and the area surrounding Basra. Here both sides concentrated their greatest efforts and marshaled the highest levels of troops and resources, with Iran hoping to score a decisive blow against Iraq by finally capturing Basra, and Iraq making a strenuous effort to contain the Iranians' advances and wear down their occupying forces.

BATTLING FOR BASRA AND THE BAGHDAD HIGHWAY

In March 1985 Iranian forces again attempted to capture control of the Basra-Baghdad highway west of the Haur al Hawizeh marshes. Doing so would have enabled Iran to sever transportation and communication links between Iraq's central command and the forces fighting in the strategically critical southern region. With over sixty thousand troops committed to the operation, Iranian forces broke through Iraqi defenses and were able to cross the Tigris River. On March 17 Iran announced it had captured the Basra-Baghdad highway, as well as all of the Haur al Hawizeh marshes south of the Iraqi town Amara. Iraq quickly rallied massive forces to push back the Iranians, mustering sixty thousand troops, including the Iraqi military's most elite units. Iraq also launched up to 250 air sorties per day against enemy positions. By March 20 Iraq had not only retaken the Basra-Baghdad highway but had pushed the Iranians back to their original positions in the marshes. The casualties from these battles were massive, with a combined total of over thirty thousand fatalities.

In September 1985 Iran launched another offensive in the Haur al Hawizeh, this one aimed at encircling Basra by expanding its control over the marsh territory. Previously, Iraqi counteroffensives had regained a large island in the western part of the marsh, but the new Iranian offensive overran the Iraqi positions, and an Iraqi counterattack failed to dislodge the enemy from their new positions. While this gave Iran the territorial gain it sought, the casualties and damage inflicted upon its forces left them too weak to subsequently stage a full-scale assault against Basra itself.

Despite the escalated violence and increasing carnage, neither side showed signs of bending, and the war continued to be "something of a deadlock," according to a British researcher at the time. He also said, "One might, however, describe the situation as a 'dynamic stalemate' . . . because there are frequent new developments and both sides want to break out of the situation they find themselves in."[59] Indeed, as 1986 started, there would be a dramatic new

Iranian soldiers pray before participating in human wave attacks against Iraqi positions in the Haur al Hawizeh region in September 1985.

IRANIAN FAO OFFENSIVE, FEBRUARY '86 TO APRIL '87

Iranian attacks

Iraqi counterattacks

0 10 20   50   100
Miles

development, as Iran would attempt to break the deadlock with a new, massive ground offensive in the south. This move would rattle Iraq and the rest of the world, as the threat of an Iranian triumph loomed again.

THE FAO OFFENSIVE

In February 1986 Iran launched a three-pronged offensive in the south that included over two hundred thousand troops. Two incursions were made to the north and south of Basra, with the third directed at the Fao Peninsula further south. This incursion was the most successful, and in fact was the greatest mili-

tary achievement made by Iran since its initial penetrations of Iraq in 1982.

Iranian forces, newly trained in innovative amphibious tactics, crossed the Shatt al Arab at several points and surprised the Iraqis during the night of February 9. Iran also launched attacks in the marshes north of Basra to divert Iraqi forces and prevent them from reinforcing those in Fao. This well-coordinated strategy, along with the massive numbers involved, enabled Iran to capture the Fao Peninsula within two days. Along with the territory, which totaled 320 square miles, the Iranians also seized massive quantities of Iraqi weapons and ammunition. The captured territory also included a missile station and a radar station used in

Iraqi air raids against targets in the Persian Gulf.

Using their newly captured Iraqi weapons as well as weapons of their own accumulated during the previous lulls in ground combat, Iran solidified its hold on Fao. Attempts to expel the Iranians during the rest of February and March again included chemical weapons attacks, but these made little headway, and Iraq suffered a higher casualty rate than in previous encounters, losing many of its best-trained soldiers. At the same time, offensives launched by the Iranians and Kurds in northern Iraq further strained Iraq's resources. By mid-March, the fierce Iraqi counteroffensives aimed at recapturing Fao had ended, but not before about thirty thousand combatants—twenty thousand for Iran and ten thousand for Iraq—had been killed. After a prolonged period without significant movement in the ground war, the Fao offensive stunned Iraq and observers throughout the world. Wright said, "The campaign's importance, psychologically as much as militarily, was unmatched since Iran's recapture of Khorramshahr in 1982. In Khorramshahr, however, Iran was only taking back what it had lost. At [Fao], Iran was on the offensive, aggressively moving into Iraq."[60]

Unable to dislodge Iran from the Fao Peninsula, the Iraqis launched a counteroffensive in May that captured sixty square miles of Iranian soil around the town of Mehran. Iraq then offered to withdraw from this territory if Iran withdrew from Fao. However, within two months Iran recaptured the territory Iraq had taken, eliminating any motivation for giving up Fao.

Iran would make additional territorial gains in the south during the next two years, enabling its forces to take up artillery positions within ten miles of Basra. This would allow Iran to maintain persistent shelling and bombardment of Basra. Yet Iran was consistently unable to actually capture Basra, which continued to be a top priority of its war strategy.

FIGHTING ON ALL FRONTS

Even as Iran gained ground in the south, its army also made significant advances in the north. In October 1986 Iranian commandos destroyed an oil pipeline that transported oil from a major Iraqi refinery in Kirkuk. In the spring of 1987, a combined Iranian-Kurdish offensive threatened to knock out a hydroelectric generator on Darbandi Khan Lake that was the principle source of electric power for Baghdad. A similar combined assault overran a military command base in the town of Arabit, also near Darbandi Khan Lake.

These developments naturally caused great alarm in Iraq. With their counteroffensives consistently thwarted or quickly turned back, Iraq resumed the War of the Cities as a means of responding to Iran's ground offensives. In January 1987 Iraq struck the Iranian cities of Tehran, Qom, and Esfahan with heavy air raids and missile strikes. Civilian casualties from these actions numbered well into the thousands. Iran responded with missile attacks against Baghdad and intensified bombing and shelling of Basra, from which by this time over five hundred thousand people had

Persian Gulf Islands Spared from Conflict

It would seem likely that the islands of Abu Musa, Greater Tunb, and Lesser Tunb, located near the Strait of Hormuz in the Persian Gulf, would have been focal points of combat action in the Iran-Iraq War. The islands were controlled by small Arab states before being seized by Iran's Shah Pahlavi in 1971. This action led Arab Iraq to break diplomatic relations with Iran, then staunchly pro-Western, and sign a treaty of friendship with the Soviet Union.

The Iraqis attacked other strategic Iranian islands close to the Strait of Hormuz during the war, and Iran had major military forces stationed on Abu Musa and the Tunb Islands. Saddam Hussein had demanded Iran vacate these islands just before the outbreak of the war. After the war started, Iraqi troops and equipment were amassed in Oman, a nation bordering on the Persian Gulf entrance to the south. Yet no assault on Abu Musa or the Tunb Islands ever came.

What prevented Iraq from attacking these islands? When the forces in Oman were discovered, many of Iraq's most powerful supporters in the war, including Saudi Arabia, Britain, and the United States, pressured Oman's ruler not to allow the attack. They considered such a military action in such a critical area too threatening to the oil shipping that was so important to the Persian Gulf States and the industrial world. Hussein was himself persuaded to call off any attempt to retake the islands from Iran, even during the height of combat action in the Gulf.

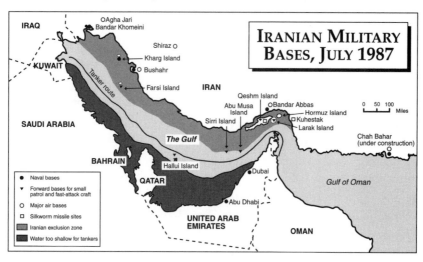

fled. The two sides again agreed to cease attacks on each other's civilian targets, but these attacks resumed in February 1988 and continued intermittently until April. Always it was Iran that sustained greater damage and casualty levels. For example, in 1988 Iraq fired two hundred long-range missiles at Iranian cities, while Iran fired seventy-seven at Iraqi targets.

Growing Global Reaction

Iraq also repeatedly used chemical weapons against the Iranians and Kurds in response to their military advances. In March 1986 the UN Security Council made its strongest statement of condemnation yet of Iraq's use of these weapons. However, the Security Council also said its members "condemn the prolongation of the conflict," and noted "that the government of Iraq has expressed its willingness to heed the call for the immediate cessation of hostilities."[61] This implied that the council was at least as concerned about the consequences of Iran defeating Iraq as it was over Iraq's chemical weapons usage. With the Security Council sending such mixed signals and taking no effective follow-up action after the condemnation, Iraq was neither hindered nor discouraged from continuing to use chemical weapons.

With bloodshed and horror seemingly spiraling out of control, the most powerful nations of the world became more active in trying to end hostilities. Going beyond providing assistance to one side, pursuing diplomatic negotiations, and maintaining defensive military forces in the area, other nations, especially the United States, involved themselves even more deeply in the war than they had in the past. This involvement would prove to be a significant factor in the war.

6 Iran and the United States Face-to-Face

The mounting destruction, catastrophic casualties, and widening frontiers of the war finally drew the world's major powers into deep and serious involvement in the conflict. In particular, a series of events during 1986 and 1987 significantly heightened concern on the part of these nations. Reflecting the ongoing fear of an Iranian victory, measures taken by the United States and other major nations similarly worked against Iranian interests and benefited Iraq. These new, more intensive intervention efforts during the last two years of the war ultimately proved to be enough to force its resolution.

KUWAIT SEEKS PROTECTION

One development that would prove to be of crucial importance occurred in October 1986, when Kuwait requested that the Soviet Union and the United States provide direct military protection for its oil tankers. This kind of security for its shipping was of critical importance to Kuwait. That nation depended wholly upon safe passage through the Persian Gulf to be able to export its oil, but its own military was inade-

quate to provide the necessary protection. The threat to Kuwaiti shipping was real; during 1985 and 1986, Iran had made fifty-five successful strikes against tankers, most of them Kuwaiti. In March of 1987, the Soviet Union complied with Kuwait's request, leasing it three oil tankers which, because they flew the U.S.S.R.'s flag, qualified for protection by Soviet military forces.

This involvement of the Soviets made the United States uneasy. The Cold War conflict between the superpowers had cooled considerably in recent years, but international competition between the two nations was not yet over. As a result, the United States looked for a way of increasing its own presence in the Persian Gulf. However, U.S. law prevented its military forces from defending any vessel officially belonging to another nation. To get around this, the U.S. and Kuwaiti governments made arrangements to have Kuwait lease half its oil tanker fleet to a private American company. These tankers would fly the American flag and receive U.S. military protection. This arrangement put American military personnel at risk, as was made vividly clear in a *U.S. News & World Report* article:

Middle East sources [say] a high-level Iranian war council in Tehran on May 10 ordered a major buildup of missile batteries and naval units at five bases along the Gulf coastline. The sources said that suicide air squadrons and mine-laying units have been put on "high alert" in apparent preparation for an increased American presence.[62]

THE IRAN-CONTRA SCANDAL

By the time the United States agreed to help Kuwait, however, American involvement in the conflict was already widely known. In November 1986, news had broken that the United States had been secretly selling arms to Iran. In a complex series of transactions, the United States had then routed proceeds of the arms sales to anti-communist forces in Central America, known as contras. Because of the involvement of the contras, the controversy generated by these secret dealings became known as the Iran-contra scandal. Exactly what motivated American officials to engage in such deals was unclear at the time, but there was evidence that the arms deals had been made in exchange for the release of American hostages being held in Lebanon by terrorists associated with the Iranians. Initially, President Reagan denied this. "My purpose was to send a signal that the United States was prepared to replace the animosity between us [and Iran] with a new relationship,"[63] he said. But in a later speech Reagan admitted "what began as a strategic opening to Iran deteriorated . . . into trading arms for hostages."[64]

In fact, the Iran-contra scandal was not the only incident of arms supplies going to Iran from nations that were either publicly for Iraq or proclaiming neutrality. In the early 1980s, a cartel of European arms suppliers had started arranging secret shipments of weapons and supplies to Iran. This cartel included companies from fourteen Western European nations, including a government-owned company in France, the nation with the most publicly pro-Iraq stance in Western Europe. As had been the case in Iran-contra, there was an alleged connection between arms shipments to Iran and attempts to free French hostages being held in Lebanon by pro-Iranian militants.

U.S. NAVAL FORCES EXPAND AND MOBILIZE

The exposure of the Iran-contra scheme had a significant impact on American policy in the Persian Gulf. In the aftermath of the scandal, the U.S. government sought to reassure its citizens and its allies that it was committed to preventing both an Iranian victory and the spread of the Islamic revolution in the Persian Gulf region. The request by Kuwait for superpower protection of its oil tankers had presented one opportunity to do this. The journal *Current History* later claimed, "Kuwait probably played on United States embarrassment to persuade the Reagan administration to accept its request"[65] for U.S. protection of its oil tankers. At the time, however, the United States cited its policy of countering any Soviet

Iran-Contra Scandal

The Iran-contra scandal, the revelation that the U.S. government was secretly selling arms to Iran to encourage the release of hostages held by Middle East terrorists, was a major problem for President Ronald Reagan and his administration. It caused credibility problems for the U.S. president both at home and with the many diverse nations that had come to support Iraq in its war with Iran. The scandal caused deep concern over the reliability of U.S. statements regarding its policy on the war.

Initially, Reagan denied that the arms sent secretly to Iran had been in exchange for the release of hostages held by terrorists with ties to Iran. However, after a special panel called the Tower Commission, which was appointed to investigate the scandal, reported its findings, Reagan admitted that he had been wrong. In fact the weapons deals had been made directly as a swap for the release of some U.S. hostages. The following excerpts are from two nationally televised speeches by Reagan on the Iran-contra scandal. The first speech was reproduced by the *New York Times* on November 13, 1986.

> "The charge has been made that the United States has shipped weapons to Iran as ransom payment for the release of American hostages in Lebanon, that the United States undercut its allies and secretly violated American policy against trafficking with terrorists.
>
> Those charges are utterly false. The United States has not made concessions to those who hold our people captive in Lebanon. And we will not. The United States has not swapped boatloads or planeloads of American weapons for the return of hostages. And we will not."

Reagan's second speech, delivered about four months later, was reproduced in the March 4, 1987, *New York Times*.

> "A few months ago I told the American people I did not trade arms for hostages. My heart and my best intentions still tell me that is true, but the facts and the evidence tell me it is not.
>
> As the Tower board reported, what began as a strategic opening to Iran deteriorated in its implementation into trading arms for hostages. This runs counter to my beliefs, to Administration policy and to the original strategy we had in mind. There are reasons why it happened but no excuses. It was a mistake."

presence in the Persian Gulf as justification for granting the Kuwaitis' request. The chairman of the U.S. Joint Chiefs of Staff at the time, Admiral William Crowe, did acknowledge that U.S. intentions in acting to protect Kuwaiti shipping were twofold: "First, to help Kuwait counter immediate intimidation and thereby discourage Iran from similar attempts against the other moderate Gulf states; and, second, to limit, to the extent possible, an increase in Soviet military presence and influence in the Gulf."[66] The subsequent buildup of U.S. naval forces in the Persian Gulf heightened tensions and anxiety over possible full-scale conflict between the United States and Iran.

President Ronald Reagan admits in a televised address that members of his staff sold arms to Iran in return for help in freeing hostages being held by terrorists linked to Iran.

Another development that served to motivate superpower involvement in the war was the discovery in February 1987, through aerial and satellite intelligence, that Iran was constructing missile launchers near the Strait of Hormuz and fitting them with extremely powerful Silkworm missiles. These weapons, obtained from the People's Republic of China, were more destructive than any missiles yet used against ships in the Persian Gulf. Simultaneous with its placement of missiles and launchers, Iran also built up its forces on islands adjacent to the strait. These Iranian moves strongly suggested that Iran was preparing to use military force to try to close off the critical Persian Gulf passage. This gave the United States strong reason to claim that it needed to bolster its forces in the Gulf to honor its commitment to keep the Strait of Hormuz open.

With an increased U.S. naval force now present, tensions in the Gulf waters were raised when, on May 17, two Iraqi Exocet missiles hit an American frigate, the USS *Stark*, resulting in the deaths of thirty-seven American sailors. Iraq claimed the missile strike was an accident and apologized, and offered both to collaborate with the United States in investigating the incident and pay reparations. The United States accepted Iraq's explanation, but acted to improve protection of its ships in the Gulf just the same. President Reagan stated that "if aircraft approach any of our ships in a way that appears hostile, there is one order of battle: defend yourselves, defend American lives."[67] With that, the po-

The guided missile frigate USS Stark *is shown burning and listing to port after being struck by an Iraqi-launched Exocet missile.*

In May 1987 U.S. warships started escorting Kuwaiti Tankers in the Persian Gulf to protect them against Iranian attacks.

tential for combat directly involving U.S. forces increased sharply.

THE UNITED STATES AND IRAN SQUARE OFF IN THE GULF

By May 1987 it was clear that no ship operating in the Persian Gulf was safe. Iran had placed mines throughout the Gulf, including in a channel leading to a major Kuwaiti oil terminal. Both a Soviet freighter and a Kuwaiti-leased Soviet tanker struck Iranian-laid mines. Another Soviet ship struck a mine in June, and on July 22 a tanker from Kuwait flying under the U.S. flag with a full U.S. military escort struck a mine near the Strait of Hormuz.

Iran showed even greater hostility toward Kuwait in September when it fired Silkworm missiles at targets on Kuwaiti soil. These missiles were fired from Iranian artillery positions in the newly captured Fao Peninsula. One missile was intended to hit an oil refinery but instead hit a nearby residential area. The Iranian government had repeatedly threatened to target Kuwait if it continued to act on Iraq's behalf. Iran's foreign minister stated that Kuwait had "virtually turned [itself] into an Iraqi province." He then asserted, "As long as Iran's oil exports are threatened by Iraq, Iran cannot allow Iraq to receive guaranteed oil [income] in order to beef up its war machine through Kuwaiti tankers flying whatever flag."[68]

Knowing the risks of attacking Kuwaiti tankers sailing under superpower protection, Iran set its sights on Kuwaiti targets not expressly protected by the Soviet Union or the United States. Still, conflict with American forces occurred, as on September 21 when the U.S. Navy destroyed an Iranian ship it claimed it had caught laying mines in the Gulf. Further direct engagement between U.S. and Iranian forces took place in early October near the heavily fortified Iranian naval base on Farsi Island in the eastern Gulf. American naval helicopters sank three Iranian patrol boats that the United States claimed had fired upon the helicopters. The conflict escalated when, after an Iranian Silkworm missile struck a U.S.-flagged tanker, the United States retaliated by destroying two offshore oil installations in the Gulf that also contained Iranian military radar and antiaircraft guns.

The conflict between Iran and the United States calmed, but the lull ended in April 1988, when the U.S. frigate *Samuel B. Roberts* sustained severe damage after striking a mine. This time the U.S. response was severe. In what Wright calls "one of the biggest U.S. military engagements since the Vietnam War,"[69] American ships destroyed two Iranian oil rigs, then sank or damaged three Iranian naval ships after being engaged by Iranian forces. Together with other damage previously inflicted by Iraqi attacks, this engagement crippled nearly half of Iran's small navy. Nearly a year after the United States and Soviet Union had interjected themselves into the Iran-Iraq War, events were turning decidedly against Iran. The United States had demonstrated that it would meet Iran head on and could inflict costly damage on Iranian forces and facilities.

IRAQI RESURGENCE

Just as Iran was finding itself confronting U.S. forces in the Gulf, its fortunes in the ongoing ground war against Iraq were also turning dramatically negative. After years of steadily losing territory and being on the defensive in the ground war, Iraq staged a surprising, stunning offensive in April 1988, using both conventional artillery and chemical weapons, that recaptured the Fao Peninsula. Iraqi troops, using helicopters and small boats, landed and attacked behind Iranian lines along the Gulf coast. Iran was taken by surprise, and within two days Iraqi forces had completely retaken Fao. This Iraqi success was a pivotal point in the ground war. Hume explains:

> The recapture of Fao was of great military and psychological significance. . . . It showed that the Iraqi army, which had been on the defensive . . . could conduct a major offensive operation with success. The victory at Fao fueled Iraqi military confidence and growing despondency in Iran over the course and costs of the war.[70]

The recapture of Fao was the first in a series of Iraqi successes over the next few months. In late May, Iraq staged successful offensives in the northern, central, and southern sectors of the front. In the south, Iraq recaptured the Shalamanche region, one of the areas surrounding Basra. In the central region, Iraq again captured the Iranian border town of Mehran during an offensive in June. They turned it over to a group of Iranian nationals known as the National Liberation Army, or the NLA. The NLA consisted of members of the Iranian opposition group Mojahaddin-i-Khalq, which had been mostly rooted out of Iran in the early 1980s. In March of 1988, the NLA had undertaken an offensive on their

IRAN-IRAQ MILITARY BALANCE, 1980–1988

	Iran 1980	Iraq 1980	Iran 1988	Iraq 1988
Force Ratio				
Regular armed forces personnel per 1000 inhabitants	6.3	18.9	13.2	63.3
Total Regular Armed Forces	246,000	242,250	644,800	1,000,000
Ground Forces				
(A) Regular Army				
Active	150,000	200,000	305,000	955,000
Reserves	400,000	250,000	350,000	0
(B) Revolutionary Guards Corps				
Active	0	0	250,000	0
Reserves	0	0	400,000	0
(C) Basij-e Mustazafin (para-military)				
Active	0	NA	350,000	NA
Reserves	0	NA	2,650,000	NA
In Service Equipment				
Battle Tanks	1740	2500	1575	4500
Armoured Fighting Vehicles	1075	2000	1800	3200
Major Artillery	1000	1000	1750	2800
Air Forces				
(A) Regular Air Force	70,000	38,000	35,000	40,000
(B) Revolutionary Guards Corps Air Units	0	NA	4800	NA
In Service Equipment				
Combat aircraft	445	335	90	484
Combat helicopters	500	40	341	232
Total helicopters	750	250	423	372
Naval Forces				
(A) Regular Navy	26,000	4250	20,000	5000
(B) Revolutionary Guards Corps Naval Units	0	NA	30,000	NA
In Service Equipment				
Destroyers	3	0	3	0
Frigates	4	1	5	1
Mine warfare vessels	0	8	5	8
Missile craft	9	12	10	8

Source: Hiro-The Longest War

own in the south-central region, with close tactical support from the Iraqis. In this operation, the NLA had captured almost four hundred square miles of Iranian territory west of Dezful. The activation of the NLA on the Iraqi side marked the greatest success Iraq had had yet in terms of forming alliances with Iranian dissidents.

Iraq also turned the tide in Kurdistan, making a swift and forceful move to retake the town of Mawet at the end of June 1988. This came on the heels of a joyous Iraqi celebration over another dramatic battlefield triumph: the expulsion of the Iranians on the Majnoon Islands. The Iraqis used the heaviest weaponry yet assembled for a single battle in the war, including two thousand tanks and six hundred artillery pieces. They also used paratroopers for the first time in the war, dropping them behind enemy positions on the Iranian side of the border. Elite units of the Iraqi military mounted an amphibious attack using hovercraft. As in the battle for the Fao Peninsula, the battle for the Majnoons was decisive and quick— Iraq triumphed in a single day.

Iraq was able to achieve these successes as a result of its massive buildup of arms and a persistent and aggressive effort to mobilize its population. While scandals in the United States and elsewhere had resulted in the drying-up of many of Iran's arms supplies, Iraq had continued to reap the full benefit of its extensive international supply network. Hiro sums up Iraqi strength leading up to their series of offensives in the spring of 1988:

> Iraq had nearly 400 combat aircraft, six times the strength of Iran's airworthy warplanes. . . . On the ground Baghdad possessed 4500 tanks and 3200 armoured fighting vehicles versus Tehran's respective totals of 1570 and 1800. Iraq owned 2800 major artillery pieces whereas Iran had only 1750. Baghdad had manged to replace its substantial losses in . . . other military hardware by continuing to borrow large sums. Its total foreign credits . . . amounted to . . . nearly three times its Gross Domestic Product. By continually extending it conscription rules Baghdad had increased its professional military troops to 955,000, far above Tehran's 655,000. Iraq's Popular Army . . . , estimated to be 650,000 strong, was slightly larger than Iran's Revolutionary Guards Corps at 620,000. Thus the Baathist regime had put under arms nearly 1.6 million men in a country with a total of 2.7 million males [of conscription age]. Its achievement looked all the more impressive in contrast to the Iranian total of approximately 1 million men under arms out of a total of some 9 million males [of conscription age].[71]

IRANIAN SETBACKS

Not only was Iran unable to obtain weapons and mobilize its population at the same levels as Iraq but a combination of damage to the nation's infrastructure and economic sanctions taken by Iraq's Arab allies had greatly weakened Iran's economy. Attacks by Iraq on both oil tankers and facilities in the Persian Gulf, as well as on oil-production facilities in Iranian cities, had actually forced the oil-rich Iran to resort to importing refined oil products starting in mid-1986. Overall, Iraq's air campaign against economic targets was so effective that the journal *Foreign Affairs* said it had "the distinction of being perhaps the sole example in history of a successful economic blockade essentially carried out by air power alone."[72]

Meanwhile, in an effort to pressure Iran into settling the war, a group of Arab oil producers, led by Saudi Arabia, had deliberately produced an oversupply of oil, driving down prices and lowering the revenues Iran could receive from its oil exports. These blows against its oil exporting capacity, as well as its overall economic isolation from world markets and the economic drain of the long and costly war

Some of the victims of Iraq's March 1988 chemical weapons attacks against Iranian civilians receive treatment.

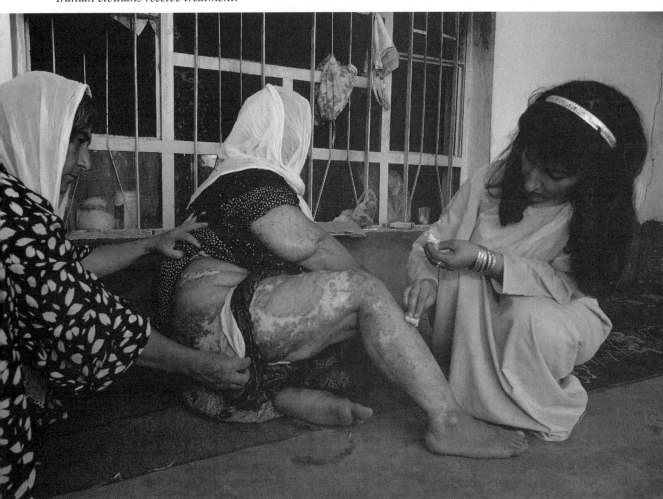

Ali Akbar Hashemi Rafsanjani

Like Ayatollah Khomeini, Ali Akbar Hashemi Rafsanjani, who served as speaker of the Iranian parliament for most of the Iran-Iraq War, came originally from a rural area of Iran. Rafsanjani was the son of a pistachio farmer from a village called Bahraman in southeastern Iran. Also like Khomeini, Rafsanjani attended the Faiziya in Qom and became an instructor there. Rafsanjani attained the title of hojatolislam, a level below that of ayatollah.

During the anti-Shah uprising of 1963, Rafsanjani was arrested and imprisoned. He remained politically active against the Shah during the years leading up to the revolution, resulting in his being arrested four more times. Khomeini appointed him a member of the Islamic Revolutionary Council, a group set up to formulate the Islamic Republic form of government for Iran. Rafsanjani was elected to the first Majlis after the revolution and gained prominence when he was elected speaker, a position he held for the rest of the 1980s. In 1990 he was elected Iran's president, a position he held until 1997.

During the time he spent in the Iranian government, Rafsanjani demonstrated strong leadership abilities. These traits had caused Rafsanjani trouble when he was in the Iranian military in 1962. His charisma and persuasive verbal skills attracted many of his fellow soldiers to his dissident way of thinking. This led to Rafsanjani being removed from the military, but over twenty years later he was to be appointed the head of the Supreme Defense Council, the governing body that had ultimate authority over Iran's military and war effort. Rafsanjani was to play a critical role in the diplomatic proceedings that led to the resolution of the Iran-Iraq War.

Ali Akbar Hashemi Rafsanjani, the speaker of the Iranian parliament, was appointed by Ayatollah Khomeini as commander in chief of Iran's military forces in the spring of 1988.

effort, meant that economic hardship was being felt widely and deeply in Iran.

At the same time Iran was hurting economically, the extremely high casualty rate being suffered by Iran's forces was lowering morale and hindering recruiting efforts. An especially gruesome chemical weapons attack in the Iraqi Kurdish city of Halabja appeared to succeed in undermining Iranian morale enough to seriously affect Iran's military recruitment. Iraq attacked the city in March 1988 after Iranian forces had taken it. Bombs containing either cyanide or nerve gas resulted in the deaths of over four thousand people, most of them civilian residents of the city. Iran broadcast photos of the victims both to their own people and the entire world, hoping to galvanize world opinion against Iraq and undermine the alliances that had strengthened Iraq's war effort. Iran's UN ambassador, Muhammad Ja'afar Mahallati, blamed previous UN inaction for Iraq's persistent use of chemical weapons, saying it had "emboldened the Iraqi rulers to increase the intensity and gravity of their crimes."[73]

The UN did react more strongly and extensively after the 1988 incident than it had previously, but ultimately, it proved unable to prevent or deter the use of chemical weapons, which continued right up until the end of the war. Moreover, Iran's publication of the photos of chemical weapons victims in Halabja appeared to have the unintended effect of frightening its own people and diminishing their willingness to continue the war. The number of new recruits, already faltering before the chemical weapons attack, dropped even more severely after the release of the photos.

SUBTLE SHIFTS IN IRAN'S STANCE

In the face of this mounting adversity, Iran gradually began to open the door to peace negotiations. The UN Security Council had recently passed Resolution 598, which included a ten-point plan for ending the war. Iran agreed with all the points in the resolution, but wanted the sixth clause, calling for an impartial investigation to determine responsibility for starting the war, to be given highest priority. While still a stumbling block, this new Iranian position provided the basis for quiet, ongoing discussions between Iranian officials and the UN.

Still, the rhetoric coming from the Iranian leadership in the spring of 1988 was strident. While addressing the Majlis after Iraq's successful offensives in the south and against Mehran, Khomeini seemed unwavering in his commitment to war. He said that Iranians "must continue their fight by depending on their faith in God and their weapons," and that "the war will be decided on the battlefields, not through negotiations."[74] Iran was conducting parliamentary elections at that time, and Khomeini advised the Iranian people to vote for candidates who were more militantly committed to Islam and against those who were more moderate in their ideology. By so doing, Khomeini implied that he favored sustaining the war effort and wanted to see people elected to the Majlis who would support that view.

Yet Khomeini also took another action that signaled a possible softening of his position: He relieved Iranian president Ali Khamenei of his duties as commander in chief of the national military and replaced him with the speaker of the Iranian parliament, Ali Akbar Hashemi Rafsanjani. This high-level leadership change indicated that, while they were reluctant to acknowledge it, Iran's leaders realized that they had serious troubles stemming from their long and painful war. Rafsanjani had hinted at this during an interview in July of the previous year. Although stating that the government was unanimous in supporting an ongoing war effort, Rafsanjani admitted that there were differences regarding how and on what level that effort should be pursued. He also acknowledged that "the high cost of the war could discourage the families of [the poor] who supply most of the troops. I have asked myself if it was opportune to ask people to tighten their belts further."[75]

FLIGHT 655 SHOT DOWN

Iran's woes were further compounded when another encounter between Iranian and U.S. forces in the Persian Gulf occurred in July 1988 that awoke combatants and observers alike to the cost of the war in the form of innocent lives. On July 3, two U.S. warships sank two Iranian speedboats after they reportedly fired at an American helicopter. With tensions heightened and the U.S. forces anticipating Iranian retaliation over this incident, crewmen on one of the warships, the cruiser USS *Vincennes,* mistook Iranian Air Flight 655 for that of an F-14 fighter. The *Vincennes* fired a missile that struck the Iranian airliner. As a result, 290 passengers and crew aboard Flight 655 died. Although president Reagan's spokesperson called the shooting "a terrible human tragedy" and said, "We deeply regret any loss of life,"[76] Joint Chiefs of Staff chairman Crow claimed, however, "based on the information currently available, the local commanders had sufficient reasons to believe their units were in jeopardy and they fired in self-defense."[77]

Iran had demonstrated its willingness to defy America and take extreme actions when confronted with hostility. Following the shooting down of Flight 655, the world held its breath, waiting to see whether the Iran-Iraq War, already horribly bloody, would take an even more destructive turn.

Chapter

7 War's Last Gasps and an Uneasy Peace

Even before the downing of its airliner, the multiple reverses Iran had suffered in its confrontation with Iraq, combined with the wide range of adverse actions taken by most of the world toward Iran, had strained to the limit Iran's resources and ability to carry on the war. Just how much the downing of Flight 655 moved Iran toward a much greater willingness to end the conflict is unclear. However, the incident did dramatically demonstrate the severe consequences Iran could bring upon itself by continuing hostilities. Soon after the airliner tragedy, Iran made a dramatic change in policy and moved to end the war through a negotiated settlement.

WIDESPREAD ALARM

In the immediate aftermath of the Iranian airline disaster, there was widespread alarm that hostilities between the United States and Iran would intensify and maybe even erupt into full-scale war. These fears were fueled when, in spite of U.S. expressions of remorse and offers to compensate victims' families, there was great outrage among Iranians. Tehran radio proclaimed, "We will not leave the crimes of America unan-

swered."[78] Ayatollah Hussein Ali Montazeri, who was widely expected to succeed Khomeini as Iran's spiritual head of state, immediately expressed fury: "If [Khomeini] gives the order . . . the cells at home and abroad will make the material, political, economic and military interests of the US the targets of their struggle."[79] However, Khomeini turned again to Rafsanjani to manage the Iranian response to the incident, and Khomeini urged Montazeri to support Rafsanjani. This was a sure sign that Iran was at last opting to pursue a peaceful settlement to the war.

TURNING TO THE UN

On July 5, Iran called for an emergency meeting of the UN Security Council. This represented a significant change in stance, since Iran had boycotted the Security Council since October 1980. In the past, Iran had felt the council was treating it unfairly and had frequently referred to it as being under the control of the superpowers. Now, however, Iran was ready to deal with the council.

Quietly, preparations began among Iran's leadership to unconditionally accept

UN SECURITY COUNCIL RESOLUTION 598

After eight long years, over a million combined casualties, and damage and destruction in the Persian Gulf region totaling in the hundreds of billions of dollars, the Iran-Iraq War was resolved when both nations accepted UN Security Council Resolution 598 in the summer of 1988. The ten principle points of the resolution sought the following objectives:

1. An immediate cease-fire and a withdrawal of combat forces to within internationally recognized boundaries

2. The formation of a team of UN observers to oversee the cease-fire and the withdrawal of troops

3. The release and return of all prisoners of war being held by both sides

4. The cooperation of Iran and Iraq with the secretary general in negotiating a comprehensive and permanent peace settlement

5. The cooperation of all other nations in the world in efforts to achieve a peace settlement

6. The formation of an impartial inquiry group to determine responsibility in initiating the conflict

7. The formation of a team of experts to study issues concerning the need for postwar reconstruction in Iran and Iraq

8. The cooperation of Iran and Iraq as well as other Persian Gulf nations with the UN in attempting to enhance security and promote stability in the region

9. Cooperation between the secretary general and the Security Council on implementing all aspects of the resolution

10. Ongoing deliberation on the part of the Security Council to ensure compliance with the resolution and subsequent peace agreements

UN Security Council Resolution 598. From July 14 to 16, top officials from the political, military, and clerical sectors of Iran's government met secretly to discuss the war and how the nation should react to the downing of their jet. The decision of those attending this meeting was to reverse Iran's previous position and unconditionally accept the UN resolution, and Khomeini concurred. In a letter received by UN secretary general

Pérez de Cuéllar on July 17, Iranian president Khamenei said that the violence of the war had "gained unprecedented dimensions, bringing other countries into the war and even engulfing innocent citizens." He went on, "Iran—because of the importance it attaches to saving the lives of human beings and the establishment of justice and regional and international peace and security—accepts Security Council Resolution 598."[80]

According to Hume, the sudden and dramatic shift in Iran's position was the result of a combination of adverse factors facing Iran, including:

The inability of the Iranian military to overcome losses suffered during the failed attack on Basra . . . the Iraqi advantage in the tanker war, especially after the U.S. entry into the Gulf; the demoralizing impact of Iraqi attacks

Iranian president Ali Khamenei (seated right) accepted the United Nations Security Council Resolution 598 because a number of adverse factors had combined to shift the military advantage in Iraq's favor.

on civilian targets during the war of the cities; the fear in the Iranian army that Iraq would again use chemical weapons; the destruction of the Iranian navy; the recent defeats of the Iranian army . . . and the nearly ten-to-one advantage Iraq now had in battle tanks.[81]

When Rafsanjani had been chosen to replace Khamenei as the head of the Supreme Defense Council, international leaders and observers had hoped that this change was being made in anticipation of Iran's unconditional acceptance of a cease-fire. As one of the few high-ranking government officials who had military experience, Rafsanjani was held in high regard by both the Revolutionary Guards and the regular military. There was concern in the government that some in the armed forces might be displeased over the acceptance of a peace offer. Rafsanjani's appointment could help ensure the acceptance of a settlement by the military and Revolutionary Guards.

KHOMEINI ADDRESSES HIS PEOPLE

It turned out that there was little dissent in the military over the decision. However, the reaction of the Iranian masses was another matter. After hearing from their government for years that the war against Iraq was a jihad that must be fought in the name of God and that compromise in such a struggle was unthinkable, many people in Iran were understandably stunned and bewildered by their leaders' sudden shift in attitude. Iran's government worried about a possible public backlash against the acceptance of the UN resolution. In speaking to the nation in a radio address on July 20, therefore, Khomeini framed the decision to accept the resolution as consistent with the national interest, Islamic principles, and the furthering of the revolution:

> The acceptance of the resolution was truly a bitter and tragic issue for everyone, particularly for me. Up to a few days ago I believed in the methods of defense and the stances anounced in the war. . . . However, due to some incidents and factors which for the time being I will refrain from elaborating on . . . and in view of the opinion of all the high-ranking political and military experts of the country . . . I agreed with the acceptance of the resolution and the ceasefire.
>
> At this juncture I regard it to be in the interest of the revolution and of the system. God knows that had it not been for the motive whereby all of us . . . should be sacrificed in the interests of Islam and Moslems, I would never have agreed to this issue. Death and martyrdom would have been more bearable to me.[82]

Khomeini also cautioned the Iranian people that "acceptance of the resolution . . . does not mean that the war has been resolved," and that Iran "must not yet regard the issue as closed."[83]

For the most part, people supported, or at least accepted, the ayatollah's statement. Among the well-to-do and upper middle

TARIQ AZIZ

Unlike in Iran, where numerous prominent political figures besides Ayatollah Khomeini emerged during the Iran-Iraq War, there were no other major political figures to emerge in Iraq other than Saddam Hussein. However, one Iraqi government official who gained international prominence during that time was Tariq Aziz.

Aziz was deputy prime minister when the war started and later became foreign minister. He played a prominent role in negotiations and diplomatic activity on behalf of Hussein's Iraqi government during and after the war. In April 1980 Aziz was the target of an assassination attempt that appeared to involve Iran. This was a key event leading up to the outbreak of war between Iran and Iraq a few months later. Aziz traveled to the United States to meet President Reagan in 1984 and formalize the resumption of diplomatic relations between the nations. He also represented Iraq at the UN during efforts to reach a cease-fire, and then in negotiations to achieve a permanent peace with Iran.

Aziz was a journalist before joining the Iraqi Baath government, where his first high-ranking position was information minister. He held that job from 1974 until 1979, when he became deputy prime minister. In 1983 he took on the role of Iraqi foreign minister, a position he held until 1991. At that time he was once again made a deputy prime minister, but continued to be active in international diplomacy. Aziz stands out among Hussein's inner ruling circle, most of whom come from the same tribal group and geographic area as he does, Tikrit, in north-central Iraq. However, Aziz comes from the city of Mosul, far to the north and west. Furthermore, Aziz is of the Christian religion, a definite minority in Iraq. Nevertheless, Aziz has managed to gain Hussein's trust and establish himself firmly within the Iraqi government's highest levels of power.

Tariq Aziz has earned the trust of Saddam Hussein and held several important positions in the Iraqi government as a result.

classes there was already strong sentiment in favor of ending the war, and the lower middle class and the poor were still personally strongly committed to Khomeini and willing to abide by his decrees, whatever those might be. Public support for ending the war was made clear by a demonstration held in Tehran on August 10, when over a million people marched to support the cease-fire's acceptance. After almost eight years of carnage and devastation, an end to the war was finally within reach.

IRAQ FIGHTS ON

It turned out Khomeini's warning that Iranians should not consider the war over when Iran accepted the cease-fire was insightful. After six years of having been far more agreeable to peace proposals than his adversary had been, Saddam Hussein responded to Iran's sudden willingness to settle the conflict with new aggression. Iraq had continued to make territorial gains in ground offensives between the time Flight 655 was shot down and Iran accepted Resolution 598. It recaptured over thirty mountain peaks in the north and drove the Iranians out of Iraqi territory in the south-central Musian region. The success of their offensive in Musian led the Iraqis to cross the border and briefly seize a town thirty miles within Iran.

Once Iran formally agreed to Resolution 598, Iraq put up other obstacles to ceasing hostilities. They insisted that direct talks between the two governments be held to resolve all issues outlined in the resolution. Iraqi foreign minister Tariq Aziz said, "It is absolutely incorrect to be hasty in taking any step before knowing the intentions of the Iranian side very accurately and comprehensively."[84] Iraq also added more conditions for its acceptance of the resolution, and in the meantime set out to seize more territory. Hussein's forces launched three more offensives simultaneously on July 22 in the northern, central, and southern border regions. And an Iraqi offensive into Khuzestan brought them to within fifteen miles of the Iranian provincial capital Ahvaz.

With Iraq's new obstructionist bargaining position and military offensives, Khomeini urged all able-bodied Iranian men to volunteer for service. It soon became clear that Iranians had heeded his words. Tens of thousands of people rushed to the front lines to face the Iraqis, in sharp contrast to the lackluster results of military recruitment efforts in the previous months. As a result, the gains Iraq realized from these final offensives were to be short-lived. By July 25, Iran had driven back the Iraqi forces approaching Ahvaz. Another Iraqi offensive in the central sector was similarly repelled by the end of the month.

Besides being thwarted in these efforts on the battlefield, Iraq was also facing additional pressures to join Iran in an unconditional acceptance of the cease-fire. Those who had allied themselves with Iraq during the war, particularly its Arab neighbors, urged it to drop its demand for one-on-one talks with Iran and the other conditions it had later added. Members of the UN Security Council, as well as the United States, Soviet Union, and the nations allied with them, also urged Iraq to

UN Secretary General Pérez de Cuéllar, following Iraq's acceptance of Resolution 598, announced that a truce would take effect on August 20, 1988.

agree to the resolution. With the UN investigating the question of chemical weapons usage in the war and due to make a report soon, Iraq faced another potential public relations problem with the nations who had befriended it during the conflict. As long as they saw Iranian revolution and extremism as a greater danger, they had been willing, however unhappily, to tolerate Iraq's use of weapons of mass destruction. With the Iranian threat now eased, they were unlikely to continue to be so tolerant.

Some observers believe that in these final weeks, Iraq badly damaged the improved standing it had gained for itself in the eyes of the world. After leaving the National Security Council, Gary Sick became a highly respected writer and authority on Persian Gulf issues. He expresses a belief that by continuing to be so flagrantly aggressive after Iran finally agreed to accept terms for peace, Iraq did a great deal to undermine itself:

> By its [reluctance] in accepting Resolution 598, by its imposition of preconditions on peace negotiations, by its unwillingness to accept the negotiating agenda of Pérez de Cuéllar, and most of all by its use of chemical weapons after Iran had accepted the cease-fire . . . Iraq managed to dissipate within a period of only a few weeks much of the support that it had managed to attract throughout the last years of the war.[85]

Faced with international pressure, Iraq relented from its demand for direct talks with Iran and also accepted Resolution 598 unconditionally. The UN Security Council approved details for implementing the resolution's provisions on August 8, and the secretary general announced August 20 as the day the truce would go into effect. Talks between representatives of the two governments would begin in Geneva, Switzerland, on August 25. However, on the day the cease-fire went into effect, Iraq occupied four hundred square miles of new Iranian territory. This was a sign of how difficult the peace negotiations would prove to be.

Death of Ayatollah Khomeini

From the time of the Iranian revolution, observers wondered what would be Iran's fate after the death of Ayatollah Khomeini. At the time of the revolution he was already seventy-six years old, and his health was declining. Nevertheless, Khomeini lived throughout the Iran-Iraq War and beyond its resolution. He finally died in June 1989.

Some predicted that Khomeini's death would plunge Iran into chaos. They believed that without Khomeini's leadership the Islamic republican government would not be able to maintain power. This concern was heightened when, a few months before Khomeini's death, Ayatollah Hussein Ali Montazeri, who had been appointed as Khomeini's successor in 1985, resigned after a dispute with Khomeini. When Khomeini fell fatally ill a few months later, there was no designated successor. However, there was enough time between the first signs of Khomeini's final illness and his death for the Iranian government's Assembly of Experts to choose another successor. They chose president Ali Khamenei to succeed Khomeini, and also proclaimed him an ayatollah. Other major figures in the Iranian government, such as the parliamentary speaker and prime minister, immediately expressed their public support for Khamenei. The prospect of a new power struggle and renewed instability in Iran was avoided.

Khomeini's funeral in Tehran attracted a crowd estimated at between 2 and 5 million. This may have demonstrated that Khomeini continued to be widely admired and even revered among many Iranians, but his funeral also revealed how much Iran had become alienated from the rest of the world. Usually, funerals of heads of state are attended by leaders from many other countries. Only one other head of state, from Pakistan, attended Ayatollah Khomeini's funeral.

Contentious Negotiations

Once the talks got under way, the two sides sparred over terms for a permanent peace settlement. Iraq stressed the importance of clearing the Shatt al Arab of debris and wreckage and demanded that Iraqi vessels be guaranteed passage through the Persian Gulf and the Strait of Hormuz.

Iraq also wanted Iran to stop detaining and searching ships in the Gulf bound for Iraq, something Iran had been doing since the summer of 1985. Iran wanted to focus on the withdrawal of forces to the international borders and the determination of the party responsible for initiating hostilities. Once again the two nations clashed over ownership of the Shatt al Arab, with Iraq claiming the 1975 Algiers Accord was null and void due to noncompliance on Iran's part. After two months the negotiations had shown such little progress that the Security Council voted unanimously to express concern over their status.

While there was no sign that a permanent peace agreement was on the horizon, Hiro claims:

There was no serious risk of the hostilities erupting again. Both nations were truly exhausted. Steeply indebted to the Gulf states, several Western nations . . . and the Soviet Union, Iraq simply did not have the freedom of action it had enjoyed eight years before. As for Khomeini, he had not initiated hostilities in the past, nor was he likely to do so now,

Grief-stricken mourners reach out to touch the body of Ayatollah Khomeini in its broken coffin during funeral services in Tehran on June 6, 1989.

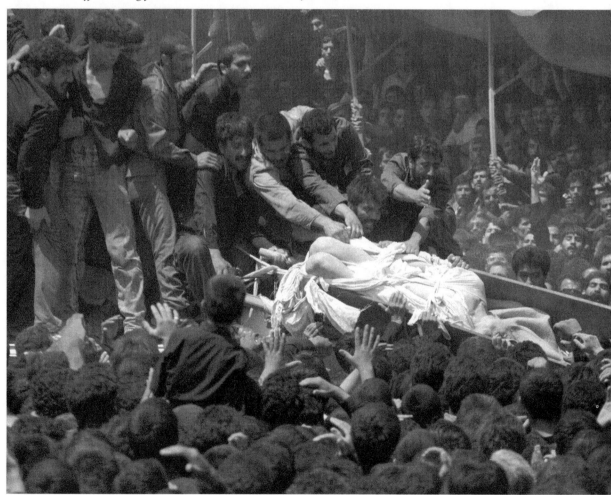

given his advanced age and poor health, and the war-weariness of his country.[86]

Nevertheless, stumbling blocks continued to hamper the peace negotiations. Early in 1989 Iranian foreign minister Ali Akbar Velayati called upon Iraq to withdraw from all the Iranian territory it was still occupying. Iraq countered with a demand that prisoners of war on both sides, totaling over one hundred thousand, be exchanged immediately. Meanwhile, international indifference toward the conflict seemed to have returned. Hume reported that "Pérez de Cuéllar had tried to involve [Security Council nations] in his negotiations, but they demurred. With the cease-fire in effect, the immediate threat to their interests had passed, and they were not eager to become reinvolved."[87]

By the time Iraq and Iran finally made their peace official in the summer of 1990,

MUSEUM COMMEMORATES IRAN-IRAQ WAR

Located in downtown Tehran, the Martyrs' Museum is dedicated to those who gave their lives in the Iran-Iraq War. Among the most dramatic—and disturbing—of the exhibits are those that include written messages and prayers by young men (some actually still only boys) who sacrificed themselves for the sake of the war.

In her book *The Last Great Revolution*, author Robin Wright describes some of the exhibits at the museum. A "petition to God" signed by fifteen soldiers reads as follows: "We pledge ourselves to become martyrs. We will fight until we die to defend our country." In fact, everyone who signed the petition died shortly thereafter.

Another display includes a letter written by a young man to his mother shortly before his death in battle. The letter reads, "Mother of mine, my martyrdom will complete your contribution to the revolution." Displays also include personal belongings recovered from the slain victims, such as bloodied garments and torn Korans that were carried into battle. A red tulip, the Iranian symbol of martyrdom, also commemorates each martyr.

There is another museum on the same block in what used to be the U.S. embassy. This museum is called the Den of Spies Center. Wright describes these two museums as "dedicated to the Islamic Republic's confrontation with the outside world."

Iranian President Mohammad Khatami (right) meets with Iraqi Foreign Minister Naji Sabri in Tehran on January 27, 2002.

Iraq was at war again, this time against Kuwait. Now at odds with nearly all of his former allies, Saddam Hussein sought to neutralize any opposition from Iran, and he showed just how quickly and radically he could shift positions when doing so served his interests. He offered to honor the territorial borders specified in the Algiers Accord, the agreement he had dramatically renounced in 1980, and also offered Iran $25 billion in war reparations. On August 21, Iraqi forces withdrew from the 920 square miles they had occupied in Iran since the cease-fire, and war prisoners were exchanged in short order.

REGION REMAINS TUMULTUOUS

In a very direct way, the conflict between Iraq and Kuwait, which was ostensibly the result of a long-simmering border dispute that dated back to the 1920s when their national borders had been drawn up by the British, was actually a consequence of the war with Iran. Following the cessation of the Iran-Iraq War, Kuwait pressed Saddam Hussein for quick repayment of the more than $12 billion in credit Kuwait had extended during the war. In essence, Kuwait was trying to use Iraq's debt as leverage to settle the old border dispute on more favorable terms. Talks between Iraq and Kuwait over these issues turned sharply bitter, culminating in Iraq's invasion and occupation of Kuwait in August 1990.

Despite the expulsion of Iraq from Kuwait the next spring by an international military alliance led by the United States, Iraq would continue to be a source of tension in the region. Furthermore, both Iran and Iraq would be implicated in supporting international terrorism after the war's conclusion, as the regimes in place at the beginning of the war remained in power. War between Iran and Iraq may not be likely again anytime soon, but both nations continue to have tense relations with each other and many of their neighbors, as well as some of the Western powers. Further conflicts in the Persian Gulf region still loom as a serious possibility for the foreseeable future.

Notes

Introduction: The Persian Gulf, Global Hot Spot

1. Robin Wright, *In the Name of God: The Khomeini Decade.* New York: Simon and Schuster, 1989, p. 86.

2. Bernard Lewis, *The Middle East: A Brief History of the Last 2,000 Years.* New York, Scribner, 1995, p. 369.

Chapter 1: Conflict Evolves and Emerges

3. Sandra Mackey, *The Iranians: Persia, Islam, and the Soul of a Nation.* New York: Dutton, 1996, p. 46.

4. Wright, *In the Name of God*, p. 43.

5. Dilip Hiro, *The Longest War: The Iran-Iraq Military Conflict.* New York: Routledge, 1991, p. 11.

6. Mackey, *The Iranians*, p. 240.

7. Mackey, *The Iranians*, pp. 239–240.

8. Quoted in "Iraq and Iran Sign Accord to Settle Border Conflicts," *New York Times*, March 7, 1975, p. 1.

9. Quoted in Matthew Gordon, *Khomeini.* New York: Chelsea House, 1987, pp. 59–61.

10. Mackey, *The Iranians*, pp. 274–275.

11. *Time*, "Man of the Year: The Mystic Who Lit the Fires of Hatred," January 7, 1980, p. 12.

12. Quoted in David Butler, et al., "Khomeini Power," *Newsweek.* February 12, 1979, p. 42.

13. Wright, *In the Name of God*, p. 37.

Chapter 2: Militants Take Power: War Breaks Out

14. Wright, *In the Name of God*, p. 86.

15. Wright, *In the Name of God*, p. 86.

16. Quoted in Gordon, *Khomeini*, p. 13.

17. Quoted in Cameron N. Hume, *The United Nations, Iran, and Iraq: How Peacemaking Changed.* Bloomington: Indiana University Press, 1994, p. 36.

18. Quoted in Wright, *In the Name of God*, p. 68.

19. Gary Sick, "Trial by Error: Reflections on the Iran-Iraq War," *Middle East Journal*, Spring 1989, p. 232.

20. Quoted in Hiro, *The Longest War*, p. 35.

21. Hiro, *The Longest War*, pp. 29–30.

22. Trevor Mostyn, *Major Political Events in Iran, Iraq, and the Arabian Peninsula, 1945–1990.* New York: Facts on File, 1991, p. 168.

23. Charles Tripp, *A History of Iraq.* Cambridge: Cambridge University Press, 2000, p. 226.

24. Quoted in "Border Agreement Ended," Associated Press, September 17, 1980.

25. Quoted in Wright, *In the Name of God*, p. 84.

26. Quoted in Bruce van Voorst, "An Interview with Khomeini," *Time*, January 7, 1980, p. 26.

27. Tripp, *A History of Iraq*, p. 232.

28. Quoted in Efraim Karsh and Inari Rautsi, *Saddam Hussein: A Political Biography.* New York: Free Press/Macmillan, 1991, p. 148.

29. Tripp, *A History of Iraq*, p. 233.

Chapter 3: Settling into Stalemate

30. Geoff Simons, *Iraq: From Sumer to Saddam.* New York: St. Martin's Press, 1994, p. 277.

31. Karsh and Rautsi, *Saddam Hussein*, p. 149.

32. Wright, *In the Name of God*, p. 103.

33. Hiro, *The Longest War*, p. 87.

34. Wright, *In the Name of God*, p. 87.

35. Quoted in Rubin, "Iran's Year of Turmoil," *Current History*, January 1983, p. 30.

36. Quoted in Shahram Chubin and Charles Tripp, *Iran and Iraq at War*. Boulder, CO: Westview Press, 1988, p. 25.

37. Hiro, *The Longest War*, p. 62.

38. Quoted in Karsh and Rautsi, *Saddam Hussein*, p. 152.

39. Hiro, *The Longest War*, pp. 92–93.

Chapter 4: Boldness and Backlash: The World Takes Sides

40. Mark A. Heller, "Turmoil in the Gulf," *New Republic*, April 23, 1984, p. 19.

41. Quoted in *Yearbook of the United Nations, 1984*, vol. 38. New York: Department of Public Information, United Nations, 1988, p. 232.

42. David Segal, "The Iran-Iraq War: A Military Anaylsis," *Foreign Affairs*, Summer 1988, p. 961.

43. Quoted in Hume, *The United Nations, Iran and Iraq*, p. 49.

44. Wright, *In the Name of God*, p. 126.

45. Quoted in Chubin and Tripp, *Iran and Iraq at War*, pp. 140–141.

46. Quoted in Simons, *Iraq: From Sumer to Saddam*, p. 284.

47. Quoted in Simons, *Iraq*, p. 287.

48. Quoted in Chubin and Tripp, *Iran and Iraq at War*, p. 208.

49. Hume, *The United Nations, Iran, and Iraq*, pp. 42–43.

50. Quoted in Hume, *The United Nations, Iran, and Iraq*, p. 47.

Chapter 5: War Frontiers Expand

51. Hiro, *The Longest War*, p. 129.

52. Quoted in Chubin and Tripp, *Iran and Iraq at War*, p. 168.

53. Hiro, *The Longest War*, pp. 131–132.

54. Richard Johns, "Kharg 'Badly Hit' in Iraqi Air Raid," *Financial Times*, September 21, 1985, p. 18.

55. Chubin and Tripp, *Iran and Iraq at War*, pp. 63–64.

56. Quoted in Chubin and Tripp, *Iran and Iraq at War*, p. 64.

57. Quoted in Claude van England, "In Iran, Opposition to Gulf War Gains a Public Voice," *Christian Science Monitor*, June 11, 1985, p. 1.

58. Quoted in England, "In Iran, Opposition to Gulf War Gains a Public Voice," p. 1.

59. Christopher Rundle, "The Iran/Iraq Conflict," *Asian Affairs*, June 1986, p. 130.

60. Wright, *In the Name of God*, p. 142.

61. Quoted in *Yearbook of the United Nations, 1986*, vol. 40. New York: Martinus Nijhoff, 1987, p. 233.

Chapter 6: Iran and the United States Face-to-Face

62. Peter Ross Range, "The U.S. Shows the Flag in Some Dangerous Places," *U.S. News & World Report*, May 25, 1987, p. 31.

63. "Transcript of Remarks by Reagan About Iran," *New York Times*, November 14, 1986, p. 8.

64. "Transcript of Reagan's Speech: 'I Take Full Responsibility for My Actions,'" *New York Times*, March 5, 1987, p. 18.

65. R. K. Ramazani, "The Iran-Iraq War and the Persian Gulf Crisis," *Current History*, February 1988, p. 61.

66. Quoted in Hume, *The United Nations, Iran, and Iraq*, p. 98.

67. Quoted in William Lowther and James Mills, "The Deadly Mistake," *Maclean's*, June 1, 1987, p. 18.

68. Quoted in Hiro, *The Longest War*, p. 188.

69. Wright, *In the Name of God*, p. 176.

70. Hume, *The United Nations, Iran, and Iraq*, p. 157.

71. Hiro, *The Longest War*, p. 195.

72. Segal, "The Iran-Iraq War," p. 960.

73. Hume, *The United Nations, Iran, and Iraq*, p. 152.

74. Quoted in Hiro, *The Longest War*, p. 207.

75. Quoted in Hiro, *The Longest War*, p. 188.

76. Quoted in John M. Broder and Melissa Healy, "U.S. Downs Iran Airliner: 290 Dead," *Los Angeles Times*, July 4, 1988, p. 1.

77. Quoted in Broder and Healy, "U.S. Downs Iran Airliner," p. 1.

Chapter 7: War's Last Gasps and an Uneasy Peace

78. Quoted in Broder and Healy, "U.S. Downs Iran Airliner," p. 1.

79. Quoted in Hiro, *The Longest War*, p. 211.

80. Quoted in Hume, *The United Nations, Iran, and Iraq*, p. 167.

81. Hume, *The United Nations, Iran, and Iraq*, p. 168.

82. *New York Times*, "Words of Khomeini: On Islam, the Revolution and a Cease-Fire," July 23, 1988, p. 5.

83. *New York Times*, "Words of Khomeini: On Islam, the Revolution and a Cease-Fire," p. 5.

84. Quoted in Hume, *The United Nations, Iran, and Iraq*, p. 170.

85. Gary Sick, "Trial by Error," p. 243.

86. Hiro, *The Longest War*, p. 253.

87. Hume, *The United Nations, Iran, and Iraq*, p. 173.

Glossary

Abadan: A city in southern Iran that is the location of the nation's largest oil refinery.

Al Daawa: A radical Shia dissident group in Iraq that staged protests, riots, and assassination attempts against Iraqi leaders.

Algiers Accord: An agreement between Iran and Iraq in 1975 that resolved territorial disputes and ended assistance by both governments to dissident groups in the other country.

ayatollah: A title denoting the highest and most revered level of Islamic clerical leadership.

Tariq Aziz: The Iraqi deputy prime minister and later foreign minister during the Iran-Iraq War; he was highly active in diplomatic and public relations efforts on behalf of Iraq.

Baath Socialist Party: A political party, including Saddam Hussein as a prominent member, that advocates Arab nationalism and economic socialism. The Baaths took power in Iraq in 1968 and have ruled the nation ever since.

Baghdad: The capital and principal city of Iraq.

Basra: Iraq's second-largest city. It is a major Shia center, key port city, and was a major target of Iranian offensives during the war.

Javier Pérez de Cuéllar: The UN secretary general for most of the Iran-Iraq War.

Dezful: A strategic Iranian city located in the southern province of Khuzestan.

Faiziya: The center of Islamic learning (*madreseh*) located in the Iranian city of Qom.

Fao offensive: An Iranian offensive launched in February 1986 that is often considered Iran's greatest ground combat success of the war. Named for the strategically critical peninsula in southernmost Iraq that was captured during the offensive.

Flight 655: The Iranian Air flight mistakenly shot down by a U.S. warship.

Gulf Cooperation Council (GCC): A group of Persian Gulf Arab nations formed in response to the breakout of the Iran-Iraq War.

Haur al Hawizeh: A marsh area in southeastern Iraq that includes the Majnoon Islands.

Saddam Hussein: The head of state of Iraq, longtime prominent figure in the Iraqi Baath Socialist Party.

Islamic Conference Organization: An international body consisting of representatives from predominantly Muslim nations.

Ayatollah Sayyed Ali Khamenei: A close follower of Ayatollah Khomeini's who was elected Iranian president in 1981 and held the position for the rest of the Iran-Iraq War.

Kharg Island: A major Iranian oil-tanker port in the Persian Gulf that was the focus of massive Iraqi attacks during the war.

Ayatollah Ruhollah Khomeini: The Iranian Shia Muslim leader who spearheaded the revolution against the Shah. After the revolution he effectively became the Iranian head of state.

Khuzestan: An oil-rich area in southwestern Iran. Previously known as Mohammera, and also sometimes called Arabistan, the region has a high proportion of Arabs, and rights to the territory have historically been the subject of Iranian-Iraqi disputes.

Kurds: An ethnic group based in northern Iraq and northwestern Iran that has historically sought independence; Kurds have often clashed with central governments in both Iran and Iraq.

Majlis: The Iranian parliamentary body, first formed in the early twentieth century.

Majnoon Islands: Strategic islands located in the marshes of southeastern Iraq.

Mojahaddin-i-Khalq: An Iranian group with an Islamic-Marxist ideology that supported Khomeini during the revolution but then took up armed opposition against the new Iranian regime.

nonaligned: Indicates a nation that sided neither with the United States nor Soviet Union during the Cold War.

Ottoman Empire: The empire based in modern-day Turkey that ruled Iraq from the fourteenth to twentieth centuries.

Qom: Generally regarded as Iran's holiest city.

Ali Akbar Hashemi Rafsanjani: A close follower of Ayatollah Khomeini's who was elected the speaker of the Majlis after the Iranian revolution and held the position throughout the Iran-Iraq War.

Resolution 598: The UN Security Council peace proposal that resulted in a cease-fire in the Iran-Iraq War.

Revolutionary Guards: An Islamic militia group that gained prominence under the Khomeini government and played a critical role in Iran's war effort against Iraq.

Shah Muhammad Reza Pahlavi: The monarchical ruler of Iran from 1941 until 1979, when he was deposed by the Islamic Revolution.

Shatt al Arab: The river that forms the Iran-Iraq border in the southernmost part of both countries and connects the Persian Gulf to the Tigris and Euphrates Rivers.

Sunni Islam: One of the two major branches of Islam, the one that makes up the minority of Muslims in both Iran and Iraq.

Shia Islam: One of the two major branches of Islam, the one that makes up the majority of Muslims in both Iran and Iraq. The Shia believe that only direct descendants of Muhammad can serve as high leaders of Islam.

Tehran: The capital and principal city of Iran.

ulama: A group of high-ranking Islamic clerics that played a major role in the Iranian revolution.

UN secretary general: The top-ranking official of the United Nations.

UN Security Council: A policy-making body of the UN that consists of many powerful nations, including the U.S.

For Further Reading

Barron's, *Islam: An Illustrated Historical Overview.* Hauppage, NY: Barron's, 2000. An advanced read, but includes ample illustrations, graphics, and sidebars, plus color-coded topics for easy reference.

J. P. Docherty, *Iraq.* Philadelphia: Chelsea House, 1999. A concise history and overview of the nation.

Elizabeth Laird, *Kiss the Dust.* New York: Puffin, 1991. Set during the Iran-Iraq War, this is a fictional account of a thirteen-year-old girl whose father's involvement with the Kurdish resistance movement in Iraq forces the family to flee, first to Iran, then to England. Offers a good historical perspective on the Kurdish situation.

Gary E. McCuen, *Iran Iraq War.* Hudson, WI: Gary E. McCuen Publications, 1987. Includes objective information about the war, various opinion pieces, and official government releases from different nations offering opposing opinions and perspectives on the war.

Don Nardo, *The War Against Iraq.* San Diego, CA: Lucent Books, 2001. Recounts the second Gulf War and provides perspective on how the Iran-Iraq War and its resolution led to further turbulence in the region.

Maria O'Shea, *Iran.* Milwaukee, WI: Gareth Stevens, 2000. Provides an overview of the history, culture, and current issues of Iran.

Rebecca Stefoff, *Saddam Hussein.* Brookfield, CT: Millbrook Press, 1995. Includes extensive biographical information on the Iraqi leader as well as good historical information on the Middle East in general and Iraq in particular.

Works Consulted

Books

Shahram Chubin and Charles Tripp, *Iran and Iraq at War*. Boulder, CO: Westview Press, 1988. Written during the final year of the war, this book focuses on the effects of the war within each country and how circumstances and conditions within each country affected their war efforts and behavior.

Frank Gibney, ed., *The Arabs: People and Power*. New York: Bantam Books, 1978. An examination of the history and contemporary issues concerning Arab peoples.

Matthew Gordon, *Khomeini*. New York: Chelsea House, 1987. A biography of Ayatollah Ruhollah Khomeini from his birth through the mid-1980s, with good background information on Islam and its various branches.

Dilip Hiro, *The Longest War: The Iran-Iraq Military Conflict*. New York: Routledge, 1991. The definitive volume on the Iran-Iraq War. One of the few books to be written specifically about the war since its conclusion.

———, *Neighbors Not Friends: Iran and Iraq after the Gulf Wars*. London: Routledge, 2001. Covers the history of the two nations and relations between them since approximately 1990; includes an overview of the postwar negotiations and how they were finally settled.

Cameron N. Hume, *The United Nations, Iran, and Iraq: How Peacemaking Changed.* Bloomington: Indiana University Press, 1994. A U.S. diplomat who participated in the United Nations' Iran-Iraq War peace efforts gives an extensive account of his experience. Events of the war itself are also recounted with fair detail.

Efraim Karsh and Inari Rautsi, *Saddam Hussein: A Political Biography*. New York: Free Press/Macmillan, 1991. A detailed biography of the Iraqi ruler and his career as a prominent national and international political figure.

Bernard Lewis, *The Middle East: A Brief History of the Last 2,000 Years*. New York: Scribner, 1995. A concise yet comprehensive history of this crucial global region; the myriad cultures, political and religious struggles, and effects of modernization are all reviewed. Includes a section on the Iran-Iraq War.

Sandra Mackey, *The Iranians: Persia, Islam, and the Soul of a Nation*. New York: Dutton, 1996. An in-depth study of historical and contemporary Iran, with a special focus on the history of struggle between rulers and masses.

Baqer Moin, *Khomeini: Life of the Ayatollah:* New York: Thomas Dunne Books, 1999. One of the more recent biographies of one of the most important and controversial religious and political leaders of the twentieth century. Includes extensive interview excerpts with close associates of Khomeini's.

Trevor Mostyn, *Major Political Events in Iran, Iraq, and the Arabian Peninsula, 1945–1990.* New York: Facts on File, 1991. A chronology of major historical events concerning nations in the region for forty-five years after World War II. Details some of the more important events during this time in the introduction, and has a separate section on the Persian Gulf War of 1991 against Iraq.

Geoff Simons, *Iraq: From Sumer to Saddam.* New York: St. Martin's Press, 1994. A broad history of the nation, with the greatest focus on its emergence as a modern nation-state, the rise of Saddam Hussein, and the recent major military conflicts that have consumed it.

Charles Tripp, *A History of Iraq.* Cambridge: Cambridge University Press, 2000. A history of the nation covering the period from the nineteenth century, when Iraq consisted of provinces of the Ottoman Empire, to the present.

Robin Wright, *In the Name of God: The Khomeini Decade.* New York: Simon and Schuster, 1989. An insightful look at Iran from the time of the revolution through the death of Ayatollah Khomeini, with extensive coverage of the Iran-Iraq War.

———, *The Last Great Revolution.* New York: Knopf, 2000. Reviews Iranian history since the 1979 revolution and analyzes contemporary conditions and developments in that nation.

Yearbook of the United Nations, 1984. Vol. 38. New York: Department of Public Information, United Nations, 1988. This annual publication covers the actions of and events pertaining to the United Nations in 1984.

Yearbook of the United Nations, 1986. Vol. 40. New York: Martinus Nijhoff, 1987. This annual publication covers the actions of and events pertaining to the United Nations in 1986.

Periodicals

Associated Press, "Border Agreement Ended," September 17, 1980.

Frederick W. Axelgrad, "Iraq and the War with Iran," *Current History,* February 1987.

John Barnes, "Truce in Troubled Waters?" *U.S. News & World Report,* August 1, 1988.

Andrew Bilski, "Fueling Iran's Fire," *Maclean's,* December 8, 1986.

John M. Broder and Melissa Healy, "U.S. Downs Iran Airliner: 290 Dead," *Los Angeles Times,* July 4, 1988.

David Butler, et al., "Khomeini Power," *Newsweek,* February 12, 1979.

William L. Chaze, "The Danger Deepens, and So Do the Doubts," *U.S. News & World Report,* August 17, 1987.

Claude van England, "In Iran, Opposition to Gulf War Gains a Public Voice," *Christian Science Monitor,* June 11, 1985.

John Greenwald, "A War on All Fronts," *Time,* August 17, 1987.

Mark A. Heller, "Turmoil in the Gulf," *New Republic,* April 23, 1984.

Jim Hoagland, "A New Ballgame in the Mideast," *Washington Post,* December 2, 1984.

Bob Horton, "Iraq vs. Iran—Who, What, and Why of a Long War," *U.S. News & World Report*, April 15, 1985.

Yousseff M. Ibrahim, "Khomeini Accepts 'Poison' of Ending War with Iraq," *New York Times*, July 21, 1988.

Richard Johns, "Kharg 'Badly Hit' in Iraqi Air Raid," *Financial Times*, September 21, 1985.

John Kifner, "Iraqi Planes Strike 10 Airfields in Iran; Oil Area Imperiled," *New York Times*, September 23, 1980.

William Lowther and James Mills, "The Deadly Mistake," *Maclean's*, June 1, 1987.

Middle East, "Too Hot to Handle," November 1980.

Gordon Mott, "Judgment on Flight 655," *Newsweek*, July 25, 1988.

New York Times, "Bakr Quits in Iraq, Name Hussein," July 17, 1979.

———, "Iraq and Iran Sign Accord to Settle Border Conflicts," March 7, 1975.

———, "Iraq Ends 1975 Border Pact with Iran as Frontier Clashes Continue," September 18, 1980.

———, "Transcript of President's State of the Union Address to Joint Session of Congress," January 24, 1980.

———, "Transcript of Reagan's Speech: 'I Take Full Responsibility for My Actions,'" March 5, 1987.

———, "Transcript of Remarks by Reagan About Iran," November 14, 1986.

———, "Words of Khomeini: On Islam, the Revolution and a Cease-Fire," July 23, 1988.

Don Oberdorfer, "Iraq Set to Renew Diplomatic Ties with U.S.," *Washington Post*, October 26, 1984.

R. K. Ramazani, "The Iran-Iraq War and the Persian Gulf Crisis," *Current History*, February 1988.

Peter Ross Range, "The U.S. Shows the Flag in Some Dangerous Places," *U.S. News & World Report*, May 25, 1987.

Steven V. Roberts, "The Reagan White House: Reagan Concedes 'Mistake' in Arms for Hostage Policy," *New York Times*, March 5, 1987.

Barry Rubin, "Iran's Year of Turmoil," *Current History*, January 1983.

Christopher Rundle, "The Iran/Iraq Conflict," *Asia Affairs*, June 1986.

David Segal, "The Iran-Iraq War: A Military Anaylsis," *Foreign Affairs*, Summer 1988.

Gary Sick, "Trial by Error: Reflections on the Iran-Iraq War," *Middle East Journal*, Spring 1989.

Hedrick Smith, "The Carter Doctrine," *New York Times*, January 24, 1980.

William E. Smith, "Clouds of Desperation," *Time*, March 19, 1984.

Philip Taubman, "Iranian Invaders Said to Penetrate 10 Miles into Iraq," *New York Times*, July 15, 1982.

Time, "An End to Isolationism," November 12, 1979.

———, "Man of the Year: The Mystic Who Lit the Fires of Hatred," January 7, 1980.

———, "The Unending Feud: Shi'ites vs. Sunnis," August 7, 1987.

———, "Unity Against the Shah," January 15, 1979.

Bernard E. Trainor, "Turning Point: Failed Attempt on Basra," *New York Times*, July 19, 1988.

U.S. News & World Report. "Iran-Iraq War: 'Now It's Hell,'" April 1, 1985.

Bruce van Voorst, "An Interview with Khomeini," *Time*, January 7, 1980.

Bernard Weinraub, "President Defends Iranian Contacts," *New York Times*, November 14, 1986.

Index

Picture Credits

Cover, Hulton Archive by GettyImages

Associated Press/Wide World Photo, 107, 109

AFP/CORBIS, 32, 101

© Bettmann/CORBIS, 19, 20, 26, 28, 30, 37, 79, 88

© CORBIS, 90

© Ed Kashi/CORBIS, 95

© Francoise de Mulder, 11, 50

© Roger Wood/CORBIS, 70

© Getty Images, 16, 34, 39, 41, 43, 45, 46, 48, 57, 59, 62, 73, 81, 91, 103, 105

Steve Zmina, 23, 35, 51, 53, 56, 65, 74, 82, 84

About the Author

David Schaffer has edited and designed books and magazines for young readers for the past seventeen years. A graduate of Skidmore College and the New York University Publishing Institute, he has written books, magazine articles, and newspaper features on history, geography, entertainment, travel, politics, and social problems confronting young people.

After spending most of his life in the New York City and Boston areas, he now lives in Upstate New York with his family.